Int

This book was written to offer guidance to those who are considering taking up a franchise as a way of starting a business. It attempts to address both the positive and negative aspects of franchising, and makes an effort to quantify the costs and potential profits of a number of specific franchises. The book does not by any means include all those franchises available — there are probably at least 300 of one sort or another. Instead it focuses on fewer than 30 superior businesses, which the author feels offer the pick of the bunch.

The studies enclosed are by no means exhaustive. Readers are advised as a matter of course to seek specialist and detailed advice on the attractiveness of a particular franchise from a qualified individual who is familiar with your circumstances. Do not invest large sums of money without taking this step.

The facts given are subject of course to change, since the franchisors are constantly changing the costs and projections of their franchise systems. You should therefore always get the most up-to-date details from the franchisor in question.

If readers have any questions or comments, they should write to the author care of Rosters Ltd, the publishers, at 60 Welbeck Street, London W1.

30 WAYS TO MAKE MONEY IN FRANCHISING

Rosters Ltd.

Other books by Luke Johnson

How To Get A Highly Paid Job In The City
(with Richard Roberts)

The Key To Making Money In The New Stock Market
(with Richard Roberts)

The Crash Of '87 And How To Profit From It

30 Ways To Make Money In Property (with Ian Gill)

30 WAYS TO MAKE MONEY IN FRANCHISING

ROSTERS LTD.

Rosters Ltd, 60 Welbeck St, London, W1.

First published in Great Britain in 1989

ISBN 0 948032 48 0

Typeset in Palatino
by JH Graphics Ltd, Reading
Printed and bound in Great Britain by
Cox and Wyman Ltd, Reading, Berks

Contents

5

Acknowledgements

The author wishes to express sincere thanks to Helen for her support and help, and the publisher Rosemary Burr for taking on this project.

This book is dedicated to Daniel, Cosmo and Sophie

The Best Franchisors

The companies profiled in this book are offering I believe the best franchise opportunities available today. They tend to have the following characteristics:

- A powerful brand name and public awareness;
- A long history of successful franchisees;
- A good number of franchisee or company-owned units operating;
- A record of growth;
- A policy of taking on new franchisees;
- Membership of the appropriate franchise trade associations.

They represent a fair spread of industries and investment levels. Clearly franchising has tended to thrive in certain fields: mostly service and retail businesses, with a majority of consumer, rather than trade operators. The restaurant and cleaning/repair businesses are well represented. Few franchises are in capital intensive businesses; most operate on high margins. In all franchises marketing plays a pivotal role. Most franchise businesses are in higher growth sectors of the economy — in some, such as fast-food catering, they are the dominant force.

Franchises have prospered in a big way in North America for decades, but were slower to catch on in the UK. Some US franchisor groups who had tried and failed at franchising their business in this country believed the British enterpreneur did not exist. But the 1980s has seen a new flowering of the enterprise spirit here, with fewer business regulations, a more favourable tax regime, and a highly pro-business government. The rate of franchising growth is now faster in Britain than the USA. The importance of franchising is illustrated by the fact that the USM — the UK's highly successful second tier stock market — has featured several major franchising businesses among its brightest stars — Body Shop, Interlink, Tie Rack are the better-known examples. The ability of the parent company to grow has been significantly helped by the potential to add on new franchised outlets.

Is Franchising Suitable For You?

A franchise business is one that should offer more security than an undertaking of your own invention. Few franchises can be started on a shoestring, but most need a maximum of £50,000 of liquid capital. Franchises do not give the all-round freedom that you will have if you run an undertaking on your own. What franchises do in essence is provide a format which works, and a name customers trust. With many independent business start-ups, the proprietor can never be sure if any sales will be made; if the costs will escalate out of control; if his resources will be sufficient to fund the business.

But with a sound franchise operation, many of the imponderables and uncertainties are removed. Experienced franchisors know which store settings are likely to succeed; they have come across most problems before, and are available to assist in crisis. Banks tend to look favourably on the larger, more legitimate franchise operations, and will frequently offer larger amounts of unsecured debt at better rates of interest than to new sole trader start-ups. The banks too rely upon the franchisor's system and their overseeing hand. Franchisees mostly benefit from economies and efficiencies of operation — thanks to their scale — which their independent rivals cannot match. This can mean greater margins and higher profits. Big scale advertising and promotions can pay off too, swamping any small ticket marketing efforts independents might launch.

Yet few franchisees in this country have really hit the big time. Although the risks are reduced, the chances of making a fortune are probably lower than if you went out on your own. There are of course possibilities to acquire more than one franchise operation, but as yet in this country they are rare, though frequent in the USA.

To work in a franchise organisation you cannot be a rebel. You must expect to conform to the tried and tested systems of the franchisor: that is after all why you started the relationship — to gain from their experience. You have to be scrupulously honest in paying the franchisor their royalty. Many franchise operations have centrally driven accounting systems partly in order that the franchisor can monitor receipts to ensure they are receiving their cut. Franchisors jealously guard their brand names and reputation, having learnt from certain pioneer UK franchise operations who found inferior franchisees and developed a poor name among customers. Such operations had to buy out the franchisees and start all over again to restablish their reputations.

This book attempts to give you the basic details regarding the 25 or so chosen franchise opportunities. I summarise the business of each and the characteristics of the various markets and trades. Detail of what the franchisor provides are covered, and the financial commitment needed. Where available I have included projections of the level of sales and profits possible. These reviews are not recommendations as such: neither I nor the publishers can guarantee that a franchise will work out if you take it on. However, I have only chosen those franchises where I think the core service/product is good, and it is possible for a franchise to do well. Have fun reading — and I hope you find a suitable franchise!

Franchises: The Basic Concept

Franchising is a highly successful commercial system imported from America which is now growing very rapidly in the UK. You buy the rights to a business format and trade mark proven by a large firm. You, as franchisee, pay the franchisor company an up-front fee and a continuing royalty based on sales; often you will also buy supplies from them, and contribute towards their central marketing fund. In return you benefit from the goodwill associated with the franchisor's name, and help in organising and managing the business.

The key selling point about franchises is that they offer potential owners a tried and tested business formula which should significantly reduce the risk of failure. Statistics from the UK and North America suggest over 85% of franchisees stay in business, while the failure rate for independent start-up small businesses as around 50% — within the first two years.

This impressive comparison needs qulification, however. As a franchisee, there are strong incentives to stay in business even if you are not making it a trading success. You are likely to have borrowed quite heavily to finance the start-up, and most of this capital would be lost if the business were shut, while the interest can be covered if the business continues to trade. As a result, many franchisees struggle along making a pathetic living, but unable to give up owing to bank obligations. Another distorting factor is the likelihood of franchisees having greater initial resources than independent business people. Franchisors check out the personal wealth of potential franchisee applicants carefully, and screen out those with minimal net worth. Yet many such individuals will set up in business on their own account — and go bust through inadequate funding.

Despite these levelling factors, it seems franchisees are able to avoid many problems which beset independent business start-ups. Valuable training is often given to franchisees, and well-developed operational systems should be supplied by the franchisor. In many cases, the brand name of the franchisee has real value — take Hertz, Body Shop and Alfred Marks to name but three. The large franchisor company may be willing to give its covenant as guarantee to the landlord when a franchisee takes on leasehold premises. With prime retail outlets increasingly sought-after, landlords normally seek a tenant with some substance and track-record — neither of which a new independent business-owner can offer. This benefit alone can in some cases be sufficient to help make the shop a success. Banks are generally more generous about the amount of finance they are willing to lend with a franchise than a purely independent start-up.

But you must be aware that if you run a franchised business you do not have total freedom. Many of the bigger (and possibly more worthwhile) franchisors are incredibly fussy about adhering to their formats and suppliers. You are indeed under contract to take their instructions, whether you think it's best or not. They take the view they know what works, and that anything else is wrong. You should therefore if you become a franchisee be prepared to take orders — of a kind. As compensation, you should be made to feel far less lonely than if you were working quite alone with an unproven business. Most problems operators encounter will have been faced before by the franchisor, and they ought to be in a position to help.

Choosing A Franchise

Deciding on which franchise to pursue is a crucial choice. The industry is still in its infancy here, and consequently there are plenty of dubious operators ready to sell you a dud format. The apparent growth of the business has inspired plenty of less impressive businesses to try franchising their format. Certain frachisors appear to be primarily in the business of selling franchises, rather than helping franchisees operate a successful business format. Such cowboys are often excellent salesmen and very persistent. The rewards after all are high — you might be asked to pay them an up-front fee of say £10,000 and further payments for supplies and equipment. You must do your own background research on a potential franchise system, to be sure that what you're buying is worth while.

There are a number of tests you can apply when appraising a potential franchisor.

1 Are they members of the British Franchise Association? If they are they adhere to certain rules of conduct, some of which protect franchisees.

2 Do they have success stories of other franchisees which they can demonstrate? Do they successfully run company-owned operations?

3 Are statistics and details available on the finances of the franchisor business? How long have they been trading, and how profitable are they?

4 Is the business a long term one, or is it a passing fad which will fade and die in due course?

5 How much money does the franchisor demand up front, and what royalty payment is expected?

6 Is a sample franchise contract available for perusal without any form of commitment?

7 Are you genuinely interested in the business, and do you have some knowledge of the field? Many franchisors say that prior knowledge of their marketplace is unnecessary. While this may be so, the greater your understanding of the particular service/production industry you're entering, the greater your chances of real success.

8 What is the initial capital requirement? Is it within your budget? Large fast-food outlets like Burger King will expect their franchisees to have liquid financial resources of at least £250,000, while at the other extreme Service-master costs less than a tenth of this figure in equity terms. Clearly you should not attempt a franchise you cannot afford. Sometimes the payback from a franchise can be slow, and you should not invest anything but money you can afford to lose — as your equity contribution.

9 Are other franchisees available to talk to? They should be able to provide an unbiased and realistic opinion about the potential profits to be made and the effectiveness of the business format. Ask them about problem areas or any disagreements, and whether their contract was restrictive. If other franchisees express dissatisfaction, you would be advised to steer clear.

10 Which areas are available to franchisees? Many of the best franchise operations have already set up in the most profitable locations, and only secondary sites are left. The well-known franchises have few really attractive opportunities still available in the London area. Some franchisors adopt the somewhat unfair policy of siting company-owned operations in the better spots, leaving the franchisees only secondary towns and shopping centres. Beware of being palmed off with an inferior site in a place you don't want to live by unscrupulous franchisors.

11 Ask about the financial background of the franchisor. A few are publicly-quoted, like Interlink and Body Shop, while other operations such as Wimpey (within United Biscuits) are subsidiaries of major multinationals. Any franchisor should be substantial and well-funded. There have been cases, such as Young's Bridal shops, where the franchisor collapsed, leaving franchisees without support and possibly owed money.

12 Even in the opening stages, check about the length of the relationship. You must not enter into a deal which requires a significant investment by you, where full profits will not be achieved for three years — and where the franchisor can terminate for any reason after five years. If you invest money on a lease premium, fittings and equipment, and build up a good trade, you must be able to extract many years of value from that outlay and effort.

13 Compare the franchise with its nearest rivals. These rivals may be franchise operations or not. Directly comparable franchises, such as Kall Kwik and American Speedy, allow a better assessment of what seems good value and likely to work. But even an amateurish comparison with non-franchise rivals is time well spent, since your operation must compete with others in the marketplace.

When analysing a franchisor, do not simply look at the company — study the marketplace too. You should for instance have doubts about entering into a franchised launderette business, since these operations are declining in number as domestic ownership of washing machines rises. And keep a close eye on the possible competition. Do not sign up for an inferior, copy-cat franchise purely because its cheaper than the number one player — you must be sure that your franchise outlet can compete in the High Street.

It can be well worth considering using a lawyer to advise you when signing a franchise contract. The best legal firms for this type of matter can be recommended by the British Franchise Association — they specialise in franchise agreements. You should check their fees with them beforehand.

Self-Analysis

Sometimes franchise relationships break down not because the franchisor's service or product is defective, but because the franchisee is not suited to running their own business — even under the umbrella of a franchise agreement.

Remember, even with the support and experience of the franchisor, you will still need to be able to:

- Work very hard — sometimes ten hours a day for six or even seven days a week — will you enjoy that? Can you spare that much time away from your family? Are you fit enough?

- Risk your time and money — do you have that much money to risk? Can you afford to lose it, if everything goes wrong? Will you be able to get work again if the business fails? What are your alternative sources of income — in employment?

Ask Yourself These Questions:

- Are you a self-starter? Even though you operate a franchise, you must ultimately shoulder the responsibilites for the business. If something has to be done, either you have to be sure it is done — or do it yourself.

- Are you enthusiastic and positive? You have to be someone who has a considerable well of optimism and self-confidence. If you lack these qualities, the inevitable set-backs the business suffers will crush you. You cannot be prone to depression or frequent bouts of illness if you're in business for yourself. Capitalism only rewards the robust!

- Do you work well with other people? If you are to manage a business with employees, and serve customers satisfactorily, you must work well with people.

The Pitfalls Of Franchising

Despite the glossy attractions of entering a franchised business, there are a number of drawbacks in many cases. The list below is a generalisation, and many factors do not apply in all cases. Taken together however, some entrepreneurs feel they are sufficient disincentive to ignore any franchise and go it themselves.

- Up front fee. This ranges from £3,000 upwards — the typical amount for a retail format might be £12,000. Most franchisors stress that they make no profit on this sum, but don't necessarily believe them. The licence fee may include various services like finding a site and negotiating the deal and offering a substantial convenant. It normally covers the cost of tuition, though in many cases 'tuition' can simply involve working in an existing branch as an unpaid assistant! It covers the handbook, which surely doesn't cost a franchisor much, and probably a batch of initial merchandise material. And of course it covers the right to use the franchisor's valuable trading name (if their trading name isn't valuable, you should forget it anyway). Be deeply suspicious of franchisors who only seem to charge a one-off fee and don't maintain much continuing involvement. They could be operating merely a pyramid scheme, and have little motivation to see that your business prospers.
- Royalties. Again there is wide variation, but most franchisors levy between 6% and 8% of turnover, excluding VAT. Generally they do not pretend to offer some kind of service for this — they argue it is their

profit etc. This method of charging a franchisee ensures at least that the franchisor is as keen as the franchisee to build sales — and it is to be hoped profits for the franchisee. Bear in mind that this royalty might represent more than the cost to you of operating a similar business under your own trading name without the discounts etc the franchisor might be able to negotiate. It shows why franchises have to be high margin businesses like catering or greeting card retailing — to allow the franchisor to take a worthwhile cut. Frequently franchisors will claim this royalty is in return for area supervisors and accounting systems. A more cynical observer might suggest franchisors monitor franchisees so closely in order to check they are not fiddling the royalty payment or selling others' goods.

- Expensive requirements. Many franchises are retail outlets, and the franchisor generally oversees the shopfitting process, insisting that only recommended suppliers are used. Such contractors are likely to be very expensive, despite the supposed subsidies some franchisors claim they make. The standard of workmanship may be good, but the price may be much more than you would have to pay a small, local firm to undertake the work. In a lot of such franchises this expenditure will be half the capital cost of the business.
- Lack of freedom. While franchisees undertake many of the risks of being in business for themselves, they do not enjoy all the flexibilites of being truly independent. Most franchisors insist on totally formatted outlets, in terms of appearance, goods sold, staff uniforms, hours open etc. Failure to comply with the franchisor's regulations means the franchisee is breaking the franchise agreement and is likely to lose the franchise. Franchisees cannot comfortably diversify within the franchise business, and they can only expand into multiple outlets if the franchisor wants them to.

- Success depends upon the franchisor. If you have done your research, you will only go into a franchise operation with sound commercial prospects — a buoyant market, popular products/service etc. But markets and businesses change. If new rivals come along, your franchisor may be unwilling to adapt and improve, and your business might suffer through the franchisor's rigidity. The best franchisors are those who spend time and money developing new products/services, combating competitors and evolving with the marketplace and their customers.
- Recommended suppliers. Many franchisors insist their franchisees use certain suppliers, or indeed receive their supplies direct from the franchisor. In theory franchisees should benefit from bulk discounts and consistent quality. In reality, all too often this obligation is simply a mechanism to give the franchisor a rake-off. If the franchisor does not actually state that no profit is made by selling items on to the franchisee, you can be sure a profit is being made — at the franchisee's expense.
- Lack of Originality. As a franchisee you will never be able to claim quite the success and respect that you would if you were a winning independent business person. As a franchisee, you win customers because of the franchise brand, not because you're behind the counter. No franchise operation ever has the name of the owner over the shopfront.

Franchising Your Business

A number of business successes have been generated by founders franchising their creation. Using the franchise route to expansion can have a number of advantages over wholly-owned operations. Generally it will be possible to get more branches established more rapidly using franchisees. Not only are they investing their money in starting each outlet, but they are contributing to the overall marketing pool which by virtue of its size will compound the firm's growth. Franchisees will be more motivated than manager employees of a big concern, since their reward relates directly to the effort they expend. Franchisees often possess local knowledge of an area which assists them in making a new operational unit work. And the national buying power which can be more rapidly obtained by franchising can save the entire group money. Most of these benefits accrue to both franchisee and wholly owned outlets.

There are of course disadvantages to franchising as opposed to conventional organic growth. Lump sum payments and royalty income will normally be less than the profits achieved if company-owned stores are successful. And it may not be possible to control franchisees as tightly as company-owned outlets. Disputes can occur and there have been cases where franchisees have rebelled and walked off. A case in point was the walk-out from Hometune, the original mobile tuning franchise, when it changed hands. The franchisees mostly did not like the terms of a new contract offered by the new Hometune owners, and 110 walked off to form Tune-Up. Another problem for many successful businesses looking at franchising is that they are putting their business reputation in other people's hands. If franchisees fail, they damage the overall credibility of the group. Historically in Britain it has been difficult to recruit sound franchisees. American firms have complained that volunteers lack the entrepreneurial skills and business acumen of their US counterparts. However, there is now the view that the revival of the enterprise spirit in Britain has stimulated more capable franchisee material to step forward.

So which businesses can be franchised? A strong and profitable business format is the basis for any franchise. The product or service must be popular, tested and of high quality — and it should be original, or at least distinctly superior to any competitors. Normally franchises are businesses serving consumers rather than businesses or industry. This is partly because franchises work through having a powerful brand name supported by a substantial national marketing budget. This type of expenditure is normally most worthwhile when selling consumer goods and services, rather than to professional buyers. Another key feature is that the system must be capable of duplication by franchisees — but not by rivals. The format should be easy to learn and operate, but protected as far as possible by patents and trademarks — and a strong brand. This last point is crucial. The really big advantage franchises have over independents is recognition among consumers. 'Wimpy,' 'Body Shop' and 'Kall Kwik' suggest credibility to passing trade, whereas sole traders can offer no such reassurance.

Franchises tend to be higher margin businesses, which allow the franchisor to cream off a healthy margin and still leave the franchisee a decent return. In printing for instance, instant print shops have been successfully franchised, partly because they charge premium prices and enjoy excellent margins. Traditional factory print workshops offer customers lower prices and consequently enjoy lower margins — and there is no room for a franchisor to take a slice of the action. In this example as in many others, the consumer pays a little more and the franchisor achieves buying economies of scale which squeeze the 5% to 10% franchisor royalty out of sales. Some franchisors charge a mark-up on goods supplied to franchisees, in addition to a royalty. If you do this it may prove more difficult to secure franchisees.

To launch a business as a franchise operation requires capital. Legal advice must be taken, and a franchise agreement drawn up. A business plan must be devised to ensure the business will make profits — both for the franchisor and potential franchisees. Not only does a pilot operation have to be established and made to work, but the systems (such as software etc) have to be developed for future franchisees. Advertising material must be prepared and items such as the handbook written and printed. And of course franchisees must be attracted, which means holding stalls at exhibitions and the marketing costs of a franchise launch. It often does not pay to accept the very first applicants, which means delaying the receipt of funds even further. Time should be taken when appraising franchisee possibles, so that only successful (and royalty generating!) franchisees result. A business infrastructure must be established to offer the on-going support which franchisees need — and pay for. Suitable suppliers must be vetted and nominated. There will be a delay before the franchisor receives revenues, since the initial franchisee fee tends to be absorbed with the expenses of that unit's setting-up. The franchisee's business will take a little while to generate sufficient sales to produce strong royalty proceeds for the franchisor. For a worthwhile franchise operation, a minimum total investment of around £250,000 is likely to be required.

Many franchise start-ups take advice from a member of the Franchise Consultants Association. They can give expert personal help to decide whether your business is capable of being franchised. They can also help you develop a franchise package. They can be especially useful in helping prospective franchisors to draw up comprehensive but fair franchise agreements, which ensure the franchisor's business is protected.

The massive commercial success of such giants as McDonalds and ServiceMaster would not have been possible without the rapid and inexpensive growth which can be achieved through franchising. For the right product or service, franchising can offer the best route to growth.

Bring Franchises Over From The USA

Introduction

Many commercial ideas spring from North America, which enjoys a highly developed economy and thousands of innovative business people. Franchising itself was pioneered there, and most new British franchises are copied from an American formula. Franchise sales in the US in 1986 exceeded $150 billion, while almost one third of all US retail outlets are franchised, while the US franchising industry as a whole employs 7 million people, almost 10% of the US working population. In America, where McDonalds fast food outlets are primarily franchised, the hamburger chain epitomises US enterprise. The emphasis in franchise operations on service and brands has mimicked US industry as a whole. Already Britain has 3,000 US franchised outlets, and each year sees several major US players arrive here. Recent start-ups included Sir Speedy Printing Centres and Tacotime.

How To Do It

There are really two methods of importing a US franchise: either the legitimate way, by agreeing a Master License or some other formal contract; or simply duplicating the idea. The second alternative is likely to be quicker and apparently cheaper. But it may lead to legal complications and prove less successful than an operation with the support of an experienced US firm. The Japanese are most adept at swiping US innovations and copying them just within the rather hazy international copyright restrictions so as not to infringe on any rights. If you decide to lift the idea, make sure it is just that, and not the name. And remember, if you are a poor imitation of the original US franchise, any success you achieve may prompt them to try Great Britain too — and with considerably more financial muscle than you. In this situation your outlets could suffer by comparison, and all you have done is carry out free market research for the US master company. This section concentrates on the first method however, since it is the proper and ultimately more efficient route.

How To Get Ideas

The very best way is to tour around and try to import those operations with which you are most impressed. Of course some business formats may not be franchised, but many of them are. To find out which US franchises are available, you need one of the many directories. Possibly the best value is Enterprise Magazines Inc's *The Franchise Handbook*, which costs just $4.95 and is published quarterly. It's available from good news-stands and contains a fairly full listing of the more serious franchisors. It has the advantage of being bang up to date. The front section includes interesting general articles on franchising topics. Another useful volume is the International Franchise Association's Directory of Membership, published annually. Two further possible volumes are the US Department of Commerce's *Franchise Opportunities Handbook*, updated at intervals, and the *Handbook of Successful Franchising*, published by Van Nostrand Reinhold.

Through any of these publications you can call and speak to whoever is in charge of international franchising and licensing. Arrange to meet with them and gauge their attitude to the idea of expanding overseas. All too often they are already in the process of tying up a deal. There are plenty of sharp, major UK firms scouring the US for strong franchising formats which they can bring to Britain. Luckily however the Americans are constantly inventive and their country is a big place. Therefore there is always a new franchise to bring over which hasn't been tried.

Bringing The Idea To Britain

You will be surprised in many cases how unimportant many Americans consider the rest of the world. When you suggest the potential scale of operations in Britain, they may well scoff — frequently they can see more units in one US state than in our whole country. However, Americans are by nature entrepreneurial, and will normally be willing to do a deal if you can show substance and credibility. The type of up-front licence fee expected will vary enormously depending on the size of the US operations and the enthusiasm the US franchisor has for overseas markets.

Become A Master Licensee

When major foreign firms wish to start franchise operations here in Britain, they will often appoint a Master Licensee as a representative and quasi joint partner. The Master Licensee will hold the rights over the franchise package in the UK and build up the business, while the originator will collect both an initial lump sum and a royalty based on performance. Most major US franchise groups started here in this manner, from Kentucky Fried Chicken to Kall Kwik (called Kwik Kopy in the US).

The local Master Licensee understands British law and business customs and has contacts and experience — especially of such complex matters as UK property. In addition, the Master Licensee believes he understands the local market best and so can suggest adaptations to the foreign-sourced franchise concept to tailor it to British customers. And it is principally the Master Licensee's money which is risked in attempting to make the franchise work in Britain. The franchise holder meanwhile keeps fairly tight control over the British operations through the licensee contract, and can end the relationship at any time by withdrawing the rights to the business systems if the terms of the contract are broken. Less management time is taken up than in say the process of recruiting agents or working full joint ventures.

There are advantages in becoming a master franchisee rather than simply attempting to duplicate a successful US operation in the UK. The US owner can provide detailed information about the business system from the inside. They can share with you their experience in coping with the various problems which crop up within the industry and with franchisees. If you work without the

US partner's approval, you risk making fundamental errors through ignorance, and delivering to your franchisees an unsatisfactory business format. Occasionally the US/foreign franchise group may be willing to put in capital to the new licensed operation. More usually however the licensee pays an up-front fee of perhaps £50,000 as a sign of substance and commitment, and a form of compensation if the project never gets off the ground.

To find out who is looking for a UK licensee, you can either canvass US franchisors directly, using publications like the *Handbook of Successful Franchising*, by Gurney & Friedlander/VNR, or you can approach various US franchise consultants who have been asked to find candidates. Occasionally you will see adverts requesting applicants for such Master Licences in papers such as the Financial Times.

Buy An Existing Franchise Outlet

Many want the enjoyment of running their own business, but not the risk. A prime reason to choose franchising as a route to self-employment is the established track record of the franchisor, and the reduced likelihood of the enterprise failing. Taking the process one step further, a would-be entrepreneur can buy an existing franchise outlet, rather than start a fresh one.

The transaction will then be with both the franchisee and the franchisor. You will have to meet the franchisee's price and gain the approval of the franchisor. Otherwise there is a possibility that the franchisor can cancel the franchise agreement and award it to an alternative operator. So buying an existing franchise unit does not of itself constitute sufficient conditions to continue the business. You will have to satisfy the franchisor as to your suitability, net worth and dedication. You may well have to undergo training so as to run the business according to the franchisor's systems.

In many other respects you should treat the deal like a conventional purchase of a private business. You should conduct a thoroughgoing investigation of the finances, verifying turnover, gross and net margins, and profits. Do not rely upon vague verbal representations from the outgoing owners. Treat filed accounts with caution, bearing in mind that such financial statements often understate profitability to lessen the tax burden. Look for major discrepancies between the actual trading figures you're provided and the franchisor's illustrative projections for the typical branch. If you lack the necessary skills to interpret profit and loss accounts and balance sheets, ask the advice of a chartered or certified accountant.

Invariably franchisee businesses will be organised into limited companies rather than trading as partnerships or sole traders. Assuming the business has been in existence for at least three years, it thus becomes compulsory to provide professionally audited accounts (although the small companies provisions of the Companies Acts reduce their usefulness) — and no excuse should be accepted for their absence.

A crucial component of many businesses is the premises. The quality of the site and the length and conditions of the lease (rarely are franchisees located in freeholds) can mean the difference between success and failure. If you are not experienced at reading leases, take it to a sound solicitor. Although his time will be expensive, it may save considerable sums. Try to determine what references the landlord will accept. In cases where the franchisor has guaranteed the lease, their wholehearted approval becomes even more essential. If the lease has plenty of time to run, determine what the rent might escalate to on the next rent review. If there is only a short length left, satisfy yourself that the landlord is willing — or will be obliged — to grant a new lease, and that the rent will not climb to uneconomic levels for the business. Remember that if the lease is drawn up outside the Landlord and Tenant Act you have minimal rights of renewal on expiry of the lease. Do not take on leases with significant contingent liabilities, such as a possibly onerous schedule of dilapidations waiting to be served upon expiry.

The other aspect of the business is the location. Most reputable franchise groups will investigate sites themselves for customer traffic, visibility etc. to ensure the required turnover can be generated. But you should independently check that enough passers-by or businesses are located in the vicinity. Ensure too that newcomer rivals have not recently set up shop in direct competition nearby and slashed trade. In many central London spots instant print shops are struggling thanks to an over-concentration of outlets: many of these franchises must be making poor returns after paying high rents.

Leading on from this, you should closely question any franchisee about why they are selling. If they come up with lame excuses, do not immediately end negotiations, but bear this in mind when listening to the vendor about other aspects of the deal. Clearly death or illness of the main proprietor is a decent reason, but always double-check with the franchisor — if they give you a reply. Some people who commence a franchise are simply not cut out for the long hours and lack the dedication. Their failure may turn into an inexpensive success for you. Depending upon the structure of the franchise contract, you may well avoid having to pay the lump sum to the franchisor, and buy a shop's fittings and goodwill inexpensively.

If the business is making healthy profits and is still growing, you can expect to pay some multiple of these. A typical franchise might achieve a 15% pretax margin before interest on sales. You could expect a multiple of between 5 and 8 times post-tax earnings, or between 1 and 1½ times sales. If the business is loss-making or barely profitable, you should base the consideration paid on assets — with possibly a premium. If the lease has a notional profit element, then you can discount the value of this to the next review or expiry and estimate the net present value of the notional cashflow. Occasionally it is possible to pick up private businesses for less than the value of the lease alone. But all too often, despite miniscule profits, the owner wants an amount for goodwill. Frequently franchise owners take on significant personal borrowings, and need to pay these off with the sale of the business. They will consequently hold out for an unrealistic price in the hope of clearing their loans. Do not be convinced by their desperation selling tactics — only pay what you genuinely believe a business is worth.

So how does one find these businesses for sale? Very often the franchisor will know exactly which franchise units might be for sale. Asking their advice as to the reasons for the sales would always be worthwhile — it could simply be that the selling owner was an inadequate businessman. But do not expect the franchisor to tell you that the reason for the business sale is the inappropriateness of the site (which the franchisor helped choose!).

Alternatively sources include newspapers — the Financial Times, Sunday Times, and Evening Standard are the best; trade journals (eg Printing World for instant print shops); specialist classified publications such as Dalton's Weekly, Exchange & Mart and London Weekly Advertiser; accountancy firms and commercial estate agents, business brokers and business transfer agencies. If you have your requirements on enough people's books, and keep looking in the various publications, you'll turn up possibilities before too long. Many believe that the best businesses are never advertised for sale. The only way you can buy these is either by knowing the owners — or by cold calling.

Overall I would not recommend you buy an existing franchise as a first step into the world of franchising. Rather, you should learn the ropes with your own franchise established from scratch, and then perhaps look to expand by buying up some of the other franchisees within your chain. Buying a successful franchise is likely to be an expensive process, since vendors rarely undersell; buying a cheap second-hand franchise operation could turn out equally costly, as there are probably good reasons for the low price.

How To Find Out About Franchise Opportunities

There are a variety of sources of information about franchises. You should absorb details from the widest possible range of publications, and study a thorough choice of different franchises before committing yourself.

The major methods of getting the facts are as follows:

1 Regular publications: there are two main magazines: *The Franchise Magazine*, published quarterly at £1.50 an issue, and Franchise World published six times a year for a fairly outrageous £35 subscription. There is also *Franchise Reporter*, a bi-monthly newsletter from the same publishing stable as Franchise World, also £35 a year. Each of these two publishers also produce an annual Franchise Directory, listing all the available franchises. They do not offer great detail or recommendations on the franchises, but suggest you contact the franchisors for further material. These books cost around £25 each. FDS publish *The Franchise Magazine* at Castle House, Castle Meadow, Norwich, NR2 1PJ, telephone 0603 620301. Franchise World are at James House, 37 Nottingham Road, London SW17 7EA, telephone 01-767 1371.

2 Material from franchisors: franchisors tend to fall into two camps: those who are actively recruiting new franchisees, and those who have long waiting lists or who have few openings. The former group predictably often include weaker propositions, while the latter category include some of the better opportunities. You will easily obtain glossy brochures and impressive projections from the former — the latter may refuse to send any material, since they are beseiged by applicants. You should study the prospectuses sent by franchisors in great depth. The more comprehensive and straightforward the original offering is, the better you can believe what the franchisor says. A prospectus should contain details of the company's track record and backgrounds of the promoters concerned. It should have a very specific breakdown of the initial financial commitment and the subsequent continuing royalties payable. It should indicate if stock has to be purchased from the franchisor. Most sound prospectuses give advice as to whether financing assistance is availabe. Many packages now include material from one or other of the major clearing banks regarding the type of support they are willing to extend. An outline of the franchise agreement should also be given, with its duration and arrangements for termination and renewal. Successful franchisors will include particulars of their existing franchise units and suggest that meetings can be fixed with franchisees to discuss the prospects.

3 Exhibitions, Conferences and Trade Shows: these are excellent venues to meet and talk with the people behind franchise operations, but many of the most attractive opportunities do not find it necessary to attend such industry events. Moreover, less worthwhile schemes are always on offer in abundance at the various annual fairs. You should not get distracted by such flim-flam merchants from sounder businesses. By all means use an exhibition to ask questions, inspect the stall and products and collect literature, but never agree to anything on the spot. Take the several offerings home and study them at leisure, away from the high-pressure sales tactics. Remember that the growth of the franchise field has drawn plenty of shysters who make money purely by receiving up-front franchise payments, and whose business formats are barely tested and ill-conceived. Such operations are effectively pyramid schemes, and may be prohibited by the 1973 Fair Trading Act. But they are often only exposed as such after many suckers have been taken in and the backers have conned the would-be franchisees out of large sums of money. You have been warned! The main annual London exhibition is the National Franchise Exhibition in London (normally Kensington) in October, while the Northern event is the British Franchise Exhibition at the NEC, Birmingham in March every year. Dresswell in London organise the first, and Acumex in Bournemouth the second. There are various much smaller regional shows held throughout the year across the country which feature certain franchise groups along with other new business venture possibilities. All these shows are advertised in advance in local and national papers and on outdoor and transport hoardings, where exact details of times and dates will be given.

4 Advertising: increasingly newspapers and magazines are carrying adverts asking for franchise applicants. Many such proposals are of minimal value; most of the better franchisors, except those just starting out, do not need to resort to such tactics to pull applicants. A recent case exposed by a Sunday newspaper involved a drink vending business where 'franchisees' were sold an operation of a batch of machines supposedly already in profitable locations. But many machines had simply been placed in offices on an initial free loan basis, and were returned once a fee was demanded by the franchisee. Consequently franchisees ended up with dozens of useless machines after having paid considerable sums in goodwill for the trading base. The up-market Sunday newspaper classified advertising sections (especially the *Sunday Times*) carry a number of franchise adverts, as do magazines such as *Exchange & Mart*, *Your Business*, and the *Daily Mail* and *Daily Express*. Some advertisers may be worth considering, but maintain a healthy scepticism.

5 Franchise Consultants: the Franchise Consultants Association lists a number of members who will for a fee offer advice about which franchise opportunity to choose. However, their words of wisdom are not cheap:

the pricier consultants charge £800 a day! Accountancy firms are a similar resource. Probably the more worthwhile accountants are those who specialise in franchising: the BFA keeps lists available if you write in. But again the cost may be prohibitive. Bank managers might well be a good source of information, since they may have banking customers who are franchisees.

6 The British Franchise Association: this is the national organisation for legitimate franchisors and professionals and banks connected with the industry. Its address is Franchise Chambers, 75a Bell Street, Henley-on-Thames, Oxon RG9 2BD. Telephone 0491 578049. It has nearly 100 members and over 50 affiliates. It can provide details of all these firms, and acts as something of a screening device, since members have to abide by a code of ethics with regard to their franchise operations.

7 Personal Experience and Word of Mouth: possibly the best source of inspiration might be a neighbourhood shopping parade. If you notice a new franchise operation and see first-hand a roaring success, you can use this direct evidence to launch with that franchise yourself. Equally you may know a franchisee who can tell you just how marvellously profitable his operations are — why not follow his lead? Of course, it pays to confirm such personal impressions with documented proof in the form of reports etc.

TNT Parcel Office

The Business

Private parcel distribution has been a growing feature of business life in the 1980s. The demand for reliable and economic — and rapid — delivery of documents and larger packages has permitted several large delivery firms to flourish — and TNT is among the largest. It is Australian-owned and has strong links with Rupert Murdoch's News International, helping to shift newspapers around the country. It now has a powerful brand name here and serves thousands of customers with everything from intra-city courier bike services to the international air courier delivery of express parcels. Recent research suggests the next-day UK parcels business alone is worth £500 million a year, while the market for 2/3 day services is valued at £600 million.

The TNT franchise sites serve as local drop-off and pick-up points for TNT customers. The franchisee helps develop the local customer base and receives a commission cheque based on a percentage of the revenue generated by the TNT parcel office. Normally these franchises are operated within an existing retail outlet — typically a garage service station — and require no stock and a minimal working capital injection, simply taking up a portion of office/shop space.

What Is Needed

TNT suggest the minimum required for a franchise is £8,500 cash. If the parcel office is being combined with an existing business, then the minimum amount is around £5,000. Working capital finance of £10,000 is also needed.

In return for this you receive an exclusive area, point of sale and marketing material, initial training, and all customer invoicing and debt collection handled by TNT. The package from TNT is offered on an initial 5 year basis. The add on package is suitably operated from a petrol filling station, a taxicab office, printshop, toolhire or car rental premises. Easy parking and fairly long opening hours are needed. There are now over 400 such TNT offices all over Britain, but they are still actively recruiting for more franchisees.

Making It Work

The usual characteristics to succeed in business are necessary: motivation, energy, and a positive attitude. Since it will be important to find new TNT customers, a willingness to go out and sell the business is also required. TNT supply you with a franchise manual and all office documentation and stationery, and help with bookkeeping. Posters, help with a van respray, window stickers and sandwich boards are all part of the deal. And of course, TNT do have a well-known brand name and one of the largest and busiest parcel distribution centres in the UK.

The Verdict

TNT's add-on Silver Package might make enormous sense for someone already running a suitable retail outlet. For a fairly modest cost it is possible to take advantage of their strong marketing presence and existing customer base with little risk and minimal extra overheads. Operating a successful TNT parcel office from a portion of your premises could generate useful extra revenue, but is unlikely on its own to provide a prosperous living. They are already fairly thick on the ground in virtually all busy metropolitan centres. So if you wish to set one up near a major town or city, you should expect to have to recruit new clients. Remember the parcel distribution business is highly competitive, and TNT is probably not the cheapest player.

More Information

Contact David Hadley,
TNT Parcel Office,
TNT House,
102 Long Street,
Athertone,
Warwickshire CV9 1BS.

Telephone: (0827) 715311

Tie Rack

The Business

Tie Rack is the only national retailer specialising in selling ties, scarves, belts and accessories. It has been franchising since 1982, and achieved a huge success on flotation on the stock market in 1987. There are now over 100 shops in the UK, and further units in the Irish Republic, France and Canada. Over 80 of these shops are operated by franchisees. The shops appeal to both men and women, and stock a wide range of high margin fashion goods – most of which are unique to Tie Rack. The accessories are generally poorly retailed in typical mens' outfitters, but offer some of the highest margins – despite the relatively low unit cost. Tie Rack shops operate effectively from small units – some only 400 sq ft large. Initially the chain prospered by specialising in providing convenience ties in London Underground units, but the product range has broadened considerably and other high traffic locations such as airports and shopping centres now offer Tie Rack outlets.

Tie Rack's focus allows it to stock a superior range of ties, scarves and similar accessories. They appeal to all age groups and classes, and seem especially attractive to tourists. It has no direct competitor, although most menswear shops stock ties. Its powerful brand name and buying strength gives it an advantage over all but the largest multiples. Marketing is unnecesssary, given the prime High Street locations.

What You Get And What It Costs

Tie Rack normally find their own sites and often pay

significant premiums for shop leases. They then fit out the branch according to their carefully thought-out colour, lighting and display criteria. Tie Rack usually spend between £50,000 and £100,000 to acquire and set-up a shop. But franchisees are normally only asked to contribute between £25,000 and £60,000 towards this capital cost. These prime locations are obtainable by Tie Rack partly because they offer a plc covenant, but also because they have in-house property expertise.

Tie Rack outlets carry relatively low stocks. The risk on stock is carried by the franchisor, not the franchisee, since Tie Rack will accept the return of merchandise within thirty days of purchase. Tie Rack makes available to franchisees a wide range of merchandise, which allow franchisees to charge competitive prices but still make healthy profits.

Franchisees are given one week's training at the Tie Rack Training School, plus a week in a franchisee's shop immediately after opening. Area managers offer ongoing support, along with the head office. Tie Rack provide brochures and leaflets and at least two sales promotion campaigns a year, with a significant continuous public relations effort. The franchise agreement is for five years.

A Tie Rack franchise costs an initial £25,000 to £60,000, depending on the location. This acts as a deposit for the shop unit, the cost of initial stocking, and an administrative fee as a partial re-imbursement of the expenses of setting up the unit. Tie Rack charges a fee based on a percentage of turnover, which covers the use of the Tie Rack name as well as rent and rates. Franchisees pay for replacement stock and everyday running costs. Tie Rack can generally achieve much higher than average sales per square foot from its smallish (400 sq ft to 700 sq ft) units than other retailers manage.

What Profits Can You Make?

Tie Rack do not provide illustrative profit projections, but an outlet with such high sales per square foot should generate at least £150,000 turnover annually, once it has become established — even from a small shop. Ties are very high margin products, and gross profits should be at least 60%. After staff, royalty, advertising and rent cost, pretax profits before drawings, interest and depreciation should be at least £30,000 from an outlet turning over £150,000.

How Can You Take It Further?

For further information you should contact:

Tie Rack plc,
Capital Interchange Way,
Brentford,
Middlesex TW8 OEX.

Telephone: 01-995 1344

Tandy

The Business

Tandy do not operate conventional franchise programmes
– they have what are called Tandy Authorised Dealers.
These are retailers who want to stock Radio Shack electronics goods and benefit from the established Tandy
name and marketing presence. There are in total 225 company owned Tandy stores in Britain and over 200
authorised dealers. They are supplied by InterTAN, the
associate of the huge US Tandy Corporation – the largest
electronics retailer in the world, with over 6,330 company-
owned outlets and 3,000 dealerships. Tandy specialise
in producing a vast array of consumer electronics items
in the Far East under a variety of in-house brands such
as 'Realistic', ranging from portable computers to
telephone connections. Dealers are offered these goods
on an exclusive basis. The company carries out fairly
extensive local and national advertising campaigns, and
produces its well-known annual catalogue and a monthly flyer programme. They supply point of sale and promotional material. They offer advice and contacts for the
smart Tandy red-and-grey store fittings. Tandy also offer
excellent after-sales service and support, including
Tandycare – a product insurance cover policy – and
repairs services.

The consumer electronics retail field has boomed in
recent years, but is highly competitive. Majors like Dixons
gain significant price and promotion advantages from
suppliers, and independents have struggled to keep up.
Joining a federation of stores like Tandy gives a retailer
high-street recognition and a ready-made range of

products. The field in general offers decent margins and a high turnover if the shop is successful. A properly run, 1,000 sq ft electronics retailer can make annual sales of £300,000 a year or more. Joining with Tandy does not mean a retailer loses his independence, since the agreement is not as all-encompassing and rigid as a standard franchise contract.

What Does It Cost?

Tandy require all dealers to be running a shop and have an interest in electronics. They should not operate within five miles of another Tandy outlet. They must make a minimum commitment to purchase an opening order totalling £3,500 and to buy Tandy merchandise to a total value of £12,000 within a twelve month period. Any dealer must contribute £500 as a 'Dealer Grand Opening' promotional fee. There is no licence fee and no royalty payment — Tandy make their cut on selling you their goods at a mark-up — but still leaving you a healthy retailer's margin.

What Do You Get?

If you wish to change your store's frontage and layout, Tandy will help you re-fit according to their outstanding corporate image, with its high profile. On their establishment all new dealers receive a grand opening advertisement placed in the dealer's biggest selling local newspaper. Tandy produce support literature, displays, price lists and a multitude of miscellaneous items annually. These include computer data sheets and an annual Christmas toy brochure. Tandy franchisees also benefit from the national advertising campaigns on TV, radio and posters. The annual catalogue is supplied to dealers and is an essential selling tool. It is available to all customers in early autumn, and is treated by many as a form of reference. A monthly 24/32 page brochure with details of new and sale products is mailed to around one million customers every month. Tandy dealers receive a free monthly point-of-sale package, including price cards for the current special offers and window posters.

Tandy products carry a guaranteed after-sales service, which means your customers should be pleased with the goods they buy. The availability of Tandycare insurance adds to this reputation.

How Do You Find Out More?

If you wish to progress this opportunity, you should contact Tandy's UK office directly for a copy of their folder. The address is:

InterTan UK Ltd.,
Tandy Centre,
Leamore Lane,
Walsall WS12 7PS.

Telephone: (0922) 710000

Spud U Like

The Business

Spud U Like operate fast-food outlets based around the concept of a baked potato filled with a choice of over twenty main items. There are take-away and eat-in facilities for customers. Spud U Like's fare is probably less calorific and more healthy than classic fried chicken, pizza or hamburger take-away meals, and certainly less expensive.

The format has been developed from its origin in Edinburgh in 1974, and now numbers over 50 branches across Britain. It is closely associated with the British School of Motoring, the largest driving school group with 180 outlets. The chain benefits from the rising tendency of Britons to eat out and the ever-greater demand for quick meals. In addition, the potato-based meals have gained approval from much of the slimming/healthy-eating lobby following the success of 'Audrey Eaton's 'F-Plan Diet'.

Running a catering establishment is a risky business (reputedly more restaurants fold — as a proportion of those started — than in any other business) and getting help from an experienced franchise group is often a sensible move. In decent locations the outgoing leaseholder will normally want a premium for their interest, and rents for catering establishments are higher than for conventional retail outlets. So the start-up finance is greater than for many new businesses — but then the rewards can be too.

What Does It Cost?

The franchisor charges an initial franchise fee of £5,000. The remaining capital items in a sample store might be:

equipment £12,000; shopfitting £28,000; signage £3,500; and other sundry start-up costs of £1,500. Including VAT of £7,500, the total start-up expense is around £57,500. This assumes an outlet of 1,000 sq ft, sufficient for 35 seats or so. Like most franchise groups Spud U Like has support from several major banks who indicate up to 70% of the capital cost can be financed. Thus the franchisee needs around £18,000 unencumbered capital to inject into the project.

Spud U Like receives a 5% royalty levied on weekly turnover, and expects franchisees to contribute 3% of turnover to an advertising fund. Spud U Like undertake regular promotions, supplemented by local advertising, to help draw customers into the outlets.

What Do You Get?

Spud U Like offer essential advice when selecting an outlet; their experience enables them to forecast how much revenue a specific location should generate. They can therefore advise whether the rent asked is affordable or not. Spud U Like undertakes cohesive advertising programmes targeted at small local markets to be implemented by the unit operators, with a heavy emphasis on promotional advertising. Spud U Like provide a comprehensive training programme, covering among other topics: food preparation techniques; equipment maintenance; hygiene; selling techniques; inventory and cost controls. Experienced staff will work alongside a franchisee's employees for the first week to show them the ropes; the cost of this is included in the franchise fee.

Spud U Like stresses the benefits of bulk buying for its franchisees. It is reckoned that the food savings alone normally outweigh the 5% royalty payment. Spud U Like also constantly updates and improves menus, as long as the new items conform to the 'value-variety-wholesome' theme which the outlets maintain.

What Can It Make In Profits?

Spud U Like's projections suggest a larger branch can achieve turnover of £150,000 plus per annum. A gross profit margin of about 66% should be achieved, leaving approximately £102,960. Overheads come to about £65,000, leaving net pretax, pre-interest, pre-drawings profits of over £37,000 — a margin of nearly 25%. This already allows for a total 8% deduction after advertising and royalty fees.

Overall Spud U Like is a fairly inexpensive fast-food franchise and the turnover is commensurately lower, but the net margin is attractive, and would represent an excellent return on money invested.

How Do You Take It Further?

You should contact Spud U Like, who will send you an information pack, which includes an application form, which you should complete and return to them if you wish to proceed. Their address and number are:

Franchises,
Spud U Like Ltd.,
34/38 Standard Road,
Royal Park,
London NW10 6EU.

Telephone: 01-965 0182

Snappy Snaps One Hour Photo Labs

The Business

This is a retail format franchise first tested in 1983 by two Kall Kwik franchisees, who understand the business of franchising from both points of view. The shops develop and print colour films and discs in just one hour. It also derives income from enlargements, film sales, photo albums, frames and cameras. In addition, labs can be fitted out with one-hour portrait studios. A Snappy Snaps Scene Machine can project on to a picture one of many hundreds of backdrops, and fine quality portrait style photos can be taken.

One hour photo labs are relatively new in this country, but most observers feel they are an explosive growth market. In the USA they now handle a large proportion of all domestic photo processing. 1987 UK consumer expenditure on all photography reached £770 million, showing 10% growth over the previous year and maintaining an expanding trend. Developing and printing accounts for 35% of all photographic spending, and film sales 24%. Falling camera costs, better and simpler cameras, more frequent holidays and rising disposable incomes are all contributing to this growth. Most projections suggest more people will want ever more photos developed in years to come. And of course they want them done quicker than ever before, and are willing to pay extra for the convenience, and to travel to locations that provide such service.

Running such a shop is a highly seasonal business, with a peak in midsummer and a smaller peak at

Christmas. Technical or photographic expertise is not necessary, since a thorough training is given.

What Do You Get?

The services offered by a Snappy Snaps outlet are fairly complete: they develop and print films and discs in one hour, they do reprints and enlargements (up to 6" ×8") in one hour, they sell batteries, frames, films and discs, and provide (externally) black and white developing, slide developing and mounting, transparencies, and prints from prints. If there is space, a one-hour portrait studio is also normally set up.

Snappy Snaps have property agents who scour the country looking for suitable properties. They will acquire properties on the franchisee's behalf where a strong covenant is necessary. They fit out the shop according to a detailed specification incorporating the powerful Snappy Snaps corporate ID. All franchisees attend a training course designed to teach the necessary product knowledge and instruction on all aspects of running your own business. Snappy Snaps Franchise owners are entitled to considerable discounts on both initial and on-going supplies and equipment. All the personalised Snappy Snaps material such as photo wallets, plastic bags etc is supplied, all promoting the shop and repeat business. Snappy Snaps help with staff recruitment, in particular the complex legal and practical requirements of staffing the franchise's lab. The corporate Snappy Snaps staff assist you in keeping the quality of your prints high and maintaining the lab chemistry. You can also be introduced to a clearing bank with whom a comprehensive finance package has been arranged. This includes a term loan and the necessary leasing finance for an equipment package. The franchise is granted for ten years, a contract which is renewed by mutual consent at the end of that period. The business can be sold to another party as long as the new franchisee is approved by Snappy Snaps.

What Does It Cost?

The cost of a Snappy Snaps unit is £92,125, excluding any possible lease premium required to buy the shop. Equipment and initial supplies cost £50,000, site acquisition costs are put at £5,000, shopfitting £12,500, franchise fee £8,000, the opening promotional launch £2,000, and a VAT and working capital allowance at around £15,000. The franchisors suggest this is financed as to £40,000 of equipment leasing, a 5 year term loan of £20,000, an equity contribution of £20,000 from the franchisee, and an overdraft of up to £15,000 for VAT and working capital. These projections do not take account of any lease premium payable, which would need to be financed separately.

The franchisor charges a 6% franchise fee on gross sales. A 2% contribution of gross sales towards the advertising and promotional account must be made. Promotional items such as window stickers, main display boards and leaflet dispensers together with corporate literature and price lists are paid for out of the national promotional account. However, Snappy Snaps are unusual in setting an annual upper limit on the franchise fee; payments due on turnover in excess of this figure are waived. This is to provide franchisees with greater motivation to succeed.

What Profits Can Be Made?

Snappy Snaps suggest a typical site should see sales climbing from an initial £75,000 annually to around £200,000 by year three. Cost of sales are approximately one third of turnover; fixed net expenses are around £45,000 annually, while variable expenses are perhaps

20% of sales. The return on sales before depreciation and interest should be £26,500 on £150,000 turnover, and £100,000 on £300,000 turnover — achievable from year 4 onwards in a successful location.

How Do You Take It Further

Snappy Snaps provide a very full and honest report on opportunities for franchisees within their system. You should write to:

Snappy Snaps (UK) Limited,
Franchise Sales,
52 Notting Hill Gate,
London W11 3HT.

Swinton Insurance

The Business

Swinton is a large chain of retail insurance brokers specialising in motor insurance. From its start in Manchester, the group has expanded to become one of the largest independent specialist motor insurance brokers, next to the AA. There are now well over 100 branches around the country, a mix of company-owned and franchised. Swinton has an excellent reputation among the public for an ability to find the most economic car insurance, partly thanks to its aggressive use of tv and press advertising and PR. Franchisees benefit from a first-class computer system for quotes and administration, as well as a central accounting function and a site leasing plan.

Nowadays customers want a warm and reliable reception from an insurance broker. Steadily rising car-ownership figures and the incidence of accidents and insurance claims mean people shop around for motor cover — which is anyway necessary by law. Insurance brokers earn commission on all premiums paid by customers through them to insurers. Rising premiums mean rising commissions. A relatively low cost structure, with minimal variable costs, mean once a broker has covered his overheads, the gross profit margin is most attractive. The capital costs are minimal, and the working capital requirements very modest. The potential for expansion is also there. Swinton's size means it receives first-class quotes from insurers and rapid responses, as well as all the latest information. Franchisees gain from all this.

Essentially Swinton is only open to those with several years of insurance experience or existing independent insurance brokers. The cost of starting a Swinton branch is relatively modest — typically less that £25,000, including shopfitting costs and £5,000 working capital. The rewards can be surprisingly high. Suggested profits for a London branch before depreciation and directors' remuneration for year three are as high as £51,000 on a £350,000 turnover. A business producing such a return could have a resale value of perhaps £200,000 — not a bad payback on £25,000!

How Much Does It Cost?

A minimum liquid sum of £7,000 is needed to start a branch. The licence fee to Swinton is a very reasonable £3,450, with a further £6,200 payable for an administration package. A shop fit for premises of around 700 sq ft Swinton estimate will cost £8,000, if no structural alterations are undertaken. A further £750 deposit on a microcomputer is required, making a grand total of £23,000 after £4,600 contribution to working capital.

In return Swinton will acquire and sub-let the office to you, provide a comprehensive operating manual, sales and promotional aids, an advertising and support programme for the branch opening, stationery and furniture and the relevant software. If you already own suitable premises, Swinton will refit them at cost in the firm's livery.

What Will I Make?

Swinton indicate that a branch in the provinces could be achieving total insurance income of nearly £300,000 per annum by the third year of trading (up from a £90,000 turnover in year one). This will be made up of premium income (about 90%), building society and life commission, and investment income. Overall net revenues should be around £85,000. Expenses in total will add up to about £37,000, giving a net profit before interest, Directors' remuneration and depreciation of nearly £50,000. A branch in the London area should be able to better that figure by perhaps 10%.

How Do I Learn More?

You should write to Swinton for a leaflet and application form:

Swinton Insurance Brokers Ltd.,
Swinton House,
6 Great Marlborough Street,
Manchester M1 5NN

The Survival Game

The Business

The survival game is an entertaining and energetic new outdoor sport which has caught on rapidly since its invention in the USA in 1981. Essentially it consists of two opposing teams aiming to infiltrate the rival's camp and steal their flag. Every player has a Splatmaster gun, loaded with harmless soluble yellow die pellets, which mark an opponent and force him out of the game. Like a mock battle, but with no real danger and played in a sporting fashion, it combines fitness skills with those of military manoeuvres. It can be played by all ages, but proves most popular among young adults. It is normally played across a large wooded field by teams of between 15 to 25 people. Judges accompany the players to ensure those shot actually retire from the game!

In 1988 the organisers expect 80,00 people across Britain to play. Survival Game (UK) Ltd currently run four centres themselves in the home counties, and there are 13 franchisees dotted around the UK from Glasgow to Devizes. The franchisor intends only to establish 25 sites nationally, as they feel this will adequately service the player market. There are several rivals, but Survival Game is probably the best known.

The game appeals to those who enjoy outdoor pursuits and a conflict without real danger. Such good natured sport allows people to release inner-City tensions without hurting others, and getting exercise and fresh air at the same time. While conscription is a thing of the past, the thrill of battle for many is strong, and the opportunity to indulge in mock skirmishes is proving highly popular.

For a franchisee it offers a pleasurable and healthy business which is now highly fashionable among smart executives as an alternative pursuit.

What Does It Cost?

The Survival Game is a relatively inexpensive franchise. Outside of the Greater London area (where the cost is 50% higher), each franchise costs £14,000 plus VAT. For this sum each franchisee receives an entire range of the necessary equipment, including 50 Splatmaster pistols and camouflage kits, along with 12,000 Splatballs and 600 carbon dioxide cannisters. Replacement equipment can be purchased on top of these quantities when needed.

The initial £14,000 lump sum gives the franchisee an exclusive eight year contract to play, promote and manage the Survival Game in a defined territory. However, franchisees must achieve a minimum level of Spatball sales to keep the territory. The Survival Game derives its ongoing income from franchisees by selling them Splatmasters and Splatballs — there is no commission or royalty charged.

In addition any franchisee must have access to a suitable piece of land — at least 30 acres of wooded area, for exclusive use and with no dangerous structures.

What Profits Can It Make

Each player pays £19.50, which includes two tubes of pellets. Survival Game suggest a successful franchisee can have 75 games over the course of a year with an average of 20 players each side, giving an effective total of 3,000 players. In addition to this £43,000 annualised game fee, there should be around £32,000-worth of paint pellets sold every year, along with £6,000-worth of CO_2 cannisters and £5,000-worth of camouflage suit hire. Overall sales in a typical unit could be of the order of £82,000. The total cost of sales would be around £30,000, giving a gross profit of approx £52,000. Overheads, including wages of judges and allowing £2,500 to rent the site, might add up to another £22,000. Thus the net pretax profits would amount to approx £30,000. This sort of profit would represent a superb yearly return on an investment of perhaps £20,000 in total — including publicity etc.

What Else Does The Franchisor Provide?

Surivival Game UK (SG) sells all the additional and replacement supplies needed to keep the game running. SG constantly market and promote the game nationally, through both public relations and advertising. They assist franchisees in deciding the lay-out etc for their sites. SG offers a full training package to the franchisee and any managers he/she employs. This includes advice on how to manage the game, keep equipment maintained, and lessons on book-keeping and accounting procedures. SG also help with the press launch. SG provide such material as the release and rental agreement which all game participants must sign. Any bookings and enquiries received by SG that cannot be most conveniently serviced through one of their wholly-owned sites is redirected to the most suitable franchisee.

What Should I Do Next?

If you think the Survival Game franchise interests you, the best idea is to play it in order to be sure you enjoy it. Assuming you do like the idea, you should contact:

Survival Game (UK) Ltd.,
South Thames Studios,
5–11 Lavington Street,
London   SE1 ONZ.

Telephone: 01-928 1733

Seekers Estate Agency

The Business

Seekers are a franchised chain of property shops. This means they do not charge a success-related fee of about 2% on sales — instead they levy a flat rate of £199.00 and no commission when a buyer is found. Thus a Seekers owner derives income from home registrations as opposed to home sales. From a start-up viewpoint, the key difference is that a property shop achieves rapid positive cashflow, since he does not have to wait until property sales are completed (which might be some months) to receive his remuneration. Such property shops have flourished in recent years alongside conventional estate agents, and Seekers has more than 70 offices in 22 counties. With home ownership in Britain now approaching 60% of all households, and people moving on average every five years — as opposed to every seven in the past — the demand for property brokers has risen strongly. Yet in areas of amazing property inflation, such as the south-east, average home sales can generate profits of several thousands of pounds for an estate agent. Many home vendors feel such a fee is too high, and prefer to use the much less expensive property shop idea. Seekers offer vendors properly produced particulars, a board, colour photographs displayed in their showroom, local advertising and trained negotiators selling homes. Seekers franchisees can also earn lucrative commissions arranging mortgages and conveyancing, while commercial property sales and business transfers are to be added to the services they offer.

Many home sellers are unused to the concept of

property shops, and suspicious that no effort will be taken to sell their home once the initial fee has been paid. The credibility and marketing muscle of a 70-strong chain counteracts this — a classic case where becoming a franchisee, rather than a pure independent — might well pay off.

What You Get And What It Costs

The one-off licence fee is £12,500, which covers your training, staff training, and the services of Seekers' staff in the setting up of an operation. You pay Seekers a fairly hefty 10% royalty on sales, and you pay in addition a 5% royalty towards a group marketing fund. In return you get the goodwill associated with the name, and ongoing support from the franchisor. As soon as the franchise agreement is signed Seekers circulate over 200 commercial and business agents with the relevant details in order to help you secure a shop. Seekers provide a full shop specification for fitting out.

The overall costs of setting up a Seekers estate agency include around £5,000 for shopfitting, solicitor and commercial agent fees for the shop premises, a launch budget of perhaps £3,000, and start-up supplies of at least £1,500 including camera, For Sale boards and stationery. Seekers indicate a minimum cash investment from the franchisee of £16,000 is required, with a total funding requirement of £32,500.

What Profits Can You Make?

Seekers franchisees derive their income from four sources: home displays; sale commission; conveyancing; and mortgages and financial services. The bulk of turnover is generated by home displays. Successful Seekers shops achieve 25 home registrations a week once they have become fully established — the record is 41 registrations in a week! On a projection of eight registrations a week

(400 a year), total revenue from all four income streams should be around £95,000. Direct sales costs will be about £22,500. Occupancy costs, including an estimated £10,000 rent, will be a further £20,000. Seekers do not allow for staff in their projections, but assume the proprietor will be the sole negotiator etc and allow £20,000 annual drawings. The net profit after such pay − but before any depreciation, lease write-off, interest etc should be over £20,000. The business is clearly a relatively low turnover, high margin affair, and is highly profitable assuming no staff are used.

What You Should Do If Further Interested

Apply to Seekers for their information pamphlet; subsequently you should contact them for an interview if you wish to progress the opportunity. Their address is:

Seekers Administration Office,
234/236 The Broadway,
London   NW9 6AG.

Telephone: 01-202 7882

Ryman

The Business

Ryman is a well-known High Street stationery chain which has been in existence since 1893. It now has over 67 shops mostly trading in the South-East, and all company-owned. Since being acquired by Pentos in 1987, it has been decided to franchise the concept, just as Pentos has successfully done with its Athena poster and card shops. Ryman has a distinctive design-led image, and is one of few multiples in a fragmented marketplace. It supplies both general and office stationery, ranging from typewriters to notepaper, offering many own-brand products on an exclusive basis. Such retail items provide the shop owner with juicy margins, sometimes as high as 40% gross profit on sale. Ryman's up-market positioning allows it to charge decent prices and distance itself from the more diversified competitors such as W.H. Smith or John Menzies.

Undoubtedly Ryman shops will fare well under the careful management of Pentos, which is achieving such success with its Dillons bookstore chain. Initial franchisees may have to overcome some teething problems as various systems are adapted to suit franchising, but they will be working with an experienced company and a proven retailing format.

Ryman's shops are presently concentrated in the South East of England, despite Pentos having a national representation through Athena and Dillons. The franchisor is keen to see Ryman's presence extend to the West, the Midlands, and the North.

What It Costs And What You Get

Starting a Ryman franchise is not cheap. Pentos estimate the initial startup cost to be about £90,000, which includes a £7,500 licence fee. Around half of this sum will be devoted to the very smart interior and shopfitting, while sundry other shop equipment and merchandise fittings cost about £21,000. Property acquisition costs and rent and rates prepayment add up to another £20,000 or so. In addition £20,000 of working capital will be necessary. Ryman levy a 7.5% commission on turnover cut on an ongoing basis as their franchise.

In return you enjoy the use of the Ryman name and corporate identity and Ryman will take on a shop lease and sub-let it to you via a 'non profit' sub-lease. The Ryman design team ensure the shop benefits from the readily noticed Ryman image. Ryman's property team are constantly scouring the country looking for suitable sites and will help you choose an appropriate trading location. There is a comprehensive training programme which all franchisees attend, schooling them in the skills and economics of retailing. Ryman provide a state-of-the-art computerised merchandise management and accounting system, which gives a franchisee total control over stock, sales and budgets. At headquarters level Ryman conduct an ongoing merchandise and marketing research and development process. This keeps franchisees supplied with valuable information about their customer base, and delivers a steady stream of profitable new items to sell. A franchisee does not have to scour the trade shows and buyers' fairs looking for original merchandise; Ryman sources a wide range of exclusive products, which give any store carrying the Ryman name an edge over the competition. And as ever, Ryman loan all franchisees the thorough manual, which details all the procedures on which the Ryman retailing system is based.

What Profits Can You Make?

Ryman provide illustrative projections which suggest turnover should rise from £250,000 in year 1 to £320,000 in year 3. This assumes a gradual increase in customer awareness, leading to a steadily increasing turnover. Trading profits will similarly climb from £18,700 to £37,000, thanks to a fairly inelastic general overhead and a gradual rise in staff costs. These projections assume a pretty steep rent and rates bill of £50,000, which should be taken to include a depreciation charge. These figures do not allow for interest costs or the proprietor's drawings. They demonstrate however that stationery and office products retailing is a high margin area, with the trading margin approaching 12% by year three.

How To Take It Further

If the idea of running a Ryman shop interests you, you should contact the Pentos Retailing Group to receive their brochure:

Pentos Retailing Group Ltd.,
Berwick House,
35 Livery Street,
Birmingham   B3 2PB.

Telephone: 021-236 6886

Pip Printing

The Business

Pip stands for 'Postal Instant Press', and is the world's largest franchise instant print shop chain. Bill LeVine, Pip's founder, invented the instant print industry by combining the new offset-litho quick access presses and the Itek platemaker camera that produced printing plates in less than two minutes. Pip started trading in Los Angeles in 1964, and in Britain in 1981. It has now more than 1,500 outlets worldwide, over 50 of them in Britain. It ranks third in size in the UK among the instant print chain, after Prontaprint and Kall Kwik.

Instant print shops are the modern retail version of the traditional jobbing printer's factory. They offer clean and convenient surroundings and use photocopiers and plastic plate offset litho, where in the past letterpress printing might have done. Prices are standardised and work is invariably done with rapid turnarounds. Most orders are smaller, short-run items from members of the public, although businesses provide a proportion of the customer base. There are at least 2,700 instant print shops in the UK, including copy shops which only do photocopying. Instant print shops rely upon high margins possible on smaller cost, quick turnaround items. Many are run by non-professional printers, since the technology is fairly straight-forward and service is considered the overriding factor in achieving success. Changes in technology such as desktop publishing and colour photocopiers are creating new opportunities. Not only do instant print shops enjoy a union- free environment; they tend to be paid in cash or on delivery, while 60 days credit to customers is normal within the traditional print trade.

Offset printing will account for over half of turnover, with design and typesetting about 15%, photocopying 20% and other items 10%. Many shops offer such services as colour, embossed, thermographed and dyeline printing, as well as selling stationery items.

Printing is a basic requirement of business and for many social purposes such as weddings and household stationery, while photocopiers have too many uses to mention. The marketplace is a resilient one and the growth of high street print shops at the expense of the old-fashioned, unionised print factory is likely to continue. Despite the growth of computers and the so-called paperless office, printed documents seem to proliferate more than ever. In addition, the growth of add-on services within print shops − turning them into business service centres − will foster further revenue sources. Facsimilie bureaus and data transmission systems are two of the ideas presently being introduced in some print shops.

What Does It Cost?

The initial franchise fee is £9,500. This covers the site acquisition costs to Pip, a training programme, a launch promotion on which Pip spend at least £2,000, and operations manual. The total typical cost of a start-up is around £80,000, of which £15,000 goes on shop fitting, £25,000 on the necessary equipment, £1,000 on stock and £25,000 on working capital. Probably £25,000 in cash is needed − the rest can be financed. In some cases applicants qualify for assistance under the Government Small Firms Loan Guarantee Scheme.

Franchisees pay Pip a management service fee of 7.5% of VAT-exclusive sales plus a contribution of 2.5% of turn-over towards advertising. The entire advertising budget is spent on promotion to help franchisees: Pip does not use this fund to pay for its internal sales and marketing overheads.

What Do I Get?

Pip provide all the usual services. There is a four-week training course. They offer site finding and appraisal resources. They take on the shop lease using their powerful covenant and sub-let to you, the franchisee. Normally premises are between 1,000 and 1,500 sq ft. You get a turnkey operation with your Pip shop. Advice is given on how the shop should be fitted, arranged and stocked. Pip designs the shop and can supervise the work. Pip is the largest buyer of instant print equipment in the world, and so achieves impressive discounts from manufacturers — all these discounts are passed direct to the franchisees. And Pip also obtains economies of scale in paper buying, an important cost of sale for any printer. As a contributor to the Pip marketing fund, you receive the benefit of big-scale advertising. A comprehensive operations manual is supplied. Pip assist with staff by making necessary arrangements for interviews, recruitment adverts, selection and training.

What Do I Do?

As the owner of the franchise, you will be involved in meeting and keeping customers happy. You will supervise employees and ensure orders are filled competently and promptly. You will canvass for new customers. You will monitor the business for pilferage and husband cash and stock, and deal with suppliers and maintenance.

What Profits Can I Make?

A medium sized print shop should turn over around £180,000 annually once established. The cost of sales is around 26%; after a 5% royalty and 5% contribution to the marketing fund, gross profit ought to be of the order of £115,000. Wages will amount to about £30,000; rent, rates and insurance perhaps another £23,000. Total overheads, including machine rentals and motor and travel should come to around £68,000. This leaves a projected net profit before proprietor's drawings and interest of over £30,000.

Where Do I Go From Here?

If you are further interested, you should write away for a brochure and application form to:

Pip UK,
Black Arrow House,
2 Chandos Road,
London   NW10 6NF.

The Big Orange

The Business

This is a simple and inexpensive franchise concept. The franchisee buys a spherical kiosk which looks like a giant split orange, and serves up glasses of freshly squeezed orange juice. The 2m wide kiosk can be sited anywhere with a healthy flow of thirsty members of the public, such as department stores, railway stations, airports and leisure centres. The unique appearance of the vending unit, and the orangematic juice squeezing machine help to attract business. Consumers are increasingly willing to pay premium prices for freshly squeezed orange juice, and are substituting this natural, healthy drink for artificial soft drinks high in sugar and caffeine. Its high Vitamin C level and nutritious value means it appeals to all age groups and nationalities. In high pedestrian traffic locations The Big Orange draws customers by virtue of being there. The Big Orange uses a unique orangematic juice squeezing machine, which allows customers to see the process. It is however a simple machine, with minimal maintenance required.

What You Need and What You Get

The total initial investment is £12,000 plus VAT to The Big Orange. In return you receive an entire package from The Big Orange. This includes full consultation, site surveys, staff training, opening assistance, the provision of business systems, as well as the supply of The Big Orange kiosk. The juicer is of course an important component, and is only available to The Big Orange franchisees. Publicity material, a cash register, and uniforms are all included in the £12.000 lump sum, along with the vital manual. Oranges too are available through The Big Orange. In addition franchisees must pay a 4% royalty to The Big Orange. The level of premium for a location is likely to be zero; stock costs are minimal, and indeed initial working capital requirements should be less than £3,000, given the cash generative nature of the business. Thus The Big Orange is one of the cheapest (in terms of total initial investment) fully fledged franchises available, but its profit projections still make juicy (excuse the pun) reading.

What Profits Can You Make?

The Big Orange project that sales in a decent location should be at least £1,000 a week, after the outlet has become established. This generates a gross annual profit of nearly £35,000, allowing for juice costing 33% of turnover. The rental and electricity allowance is around £8,000 (15% of turnover), with wages a similar amount annually. The projected profit before tax after a 10% depreciation charge is nearly £12,000 a year. The Big Orange projects that this could rise to nearly £25,000 on annual sales of £100,000.

The Big Orange seem agreeable to multiple franchisees if they prove they have the ability and resources after making a single operation work successfully.

How Do I Find Out More?

If you feel this franchise is of interest, you should write to The Big Orange for their brochure and background specifics.

The Big Orange (Promotions) Ltd.
18a Parade Road,
St. Helier,
Jersey,
Channel Islands.

Telephone: (0534) 77021

Midas Brake and Exhaust Centres

What Is It?

Midas is a massive worldwide franchise operation selling car brake and exhaust systems. It began as a single shop in Macon, Georgia in 1955; Midas stood for 'Muffler Installer Dealer Associated Services'. It is now the world's largest exhaust and brake specialist, with a network of over 2,000 shops throughout the USA, Canada, Australia, Mexico and Western Europe. It currently operates a chain of more than 50 shops in Britain.

As a franchise it is available either as an add-on to an existing operation for a garage owner, or as a start-up. Alternatively, a franchisee can buy into an existing centre — although one is always tempted to ask — why are they selling?

Midas has a long list of new towns where they wish to locate Midas Centres. Each region should have a catchment area of over 50,000 people, and each outlet should be on a busy main road location, with ease of access and parking. Anywhere in size between 3,500 sq ft and 10,000 sq ft will be considered, as long as the garage (or vacant lot) has a minimum 50 foot frontage. Working headroom of 12 feet is necessary, as is a basic comfortable customer reception area. There should be potential for projecting and illuminated signage. Both greenfield locations and those needing conversion will be considered.

In addition to exhaust and brake systems checks, repairs and replacements, Midas offer suspension and tyre service. They compete in the massive car repairs market with conventional service garages and chains such as Kwik-Fit. With an ever-growing pool of used cars needing to be kept running, the demand for rapidly wearing car components such as brakes and exhausts rises every year. Midas enjoys a strong brand name which carries credibility in a marketplace littered with cowboys and disenchanted customers. The Midas philosophy of serving customers properly is in stark contrast to many garage owners' methods of operation, and gets Midas business others may well miss. The training and experience of providing more exhausts than anyone else can make this a very worthwhile franchise.

What Does It Cost?

Like virtually all franchisors, Midas extract a once-only fee for joining the club, and a royalty payment on a continuing basis. The franchise fee is £10,000, while the royalty is 6%. Investment in repair shop equipment is a further £3,500, with a substantial £35,000 expenditure on fitting the centre out. Stock will cost around £25,000 (but will be sold in the course of business), while the signage will cost £2,500. Legal and professional fees will amount to about £3,000. The overall capital establishment cost is typically £80,000, although it varies according to any premium payable and the size of the outlet.

An average Midas outlet should achieve sales of perhaps £215,000 annually, equating to over £4,000 a week. The gross margin is around 60%, with variable expenses of perhaps 35% of sales and fixed expenses a further 13% of sales. This gives a gross operating profit of around 11% or nearly £25,000 per annum. Over time such a sales figure should rise once a centre has become fully established.

What Do I Get?

Midas offers a household name in its particular car repair niche. Customer familiarity will bring business. Midas will help choose and appraise your site, with specialist surveyors, solicitors, and engineers. The franchisor will provide suitable introductions to a bank to raise the loan to help finance perhaps two-thirds of the start-up cost of the business. Midas provides comprehensive financial projections as part of the bank presentation. As a franchisee, you and your staff will receive a full training in competent exhaust and brake servicing, including a certificate from Midas's national training centre. Midas negotiate keen prices with exhaust, shocks, tyre and brake part manufacturers, the benefit of which is passed on to franchisees. They provide franchisees with a simple-to-use customised computer system that handles customer accounts, stock control and pricing. This also allows Midas to monitor you via their central computer! Midas undertake national and local advertising and PR campaigns which benefit their franchisees. Again, Midas use a substantial advertising agency which negotiates finer advertising rates than an independent would be able to obtain. Midas also has block bookings with Yellow Pages and Thomson Directories.

Where Do I Go From Here?

If you have further interest, you should apply to Midas to fill out an application form. Their address is:

Midas (Great Britain) Ltd.,
107 Mortlake High Street,
London SW14 8HH.

Telephone: 01-878 9951

Knobs & Knockers

The Business

This is a company-owned and franchise chain of shops specialising in internal and external door furniture in brass, black iron and porcelain, together with co-ordinating brass light switches, dimmers and sockets. It has proved very successful and now has over 50 branches. Shares in the business were floated on the stock market in 1987. The growth of interest in high quality and antique home interiors has fuelled Knobs & Knockers achievements. Its upmarket and distinctive image appeals to the DIY home decorator and building trade contractors who require more sophisticated metal door furniture and accessories. The chain has developed many exclusive designs including lamps, fireplaces, clocks and picture frames. There is a Contract & Trade Division which supplies architects, designers, builders and developers on a trade basis.

What You Get

Knobs & Knockers is the market leader within its retail niche, and its memorable name will give franchisees instant recognition amongst customers. Since over 70% of the chain's products are exclusive, franchisees will obtain a much more varied range of merchandise to sell than if they tried operating independently. Knobs & Knockers now has over 1,000 products, and the list continues to grow. The franchisor has smart and efficient shop design specifications which present the products in the most appealing way and encourage sales.

Since Knobs & Knockers has its own London

warehouse, franchisees receive frequent deliveries of stock. Consequently the shops need keep minimum levels of stock, so reducing working capital requirements and storage problems. The chain's bulk purchasing power ensures that the franchisees only sell value for money products. Meanwhile new products are being constantly introduced, all of which have been pre-tested within company-owned locations.

What Does It Cost?

The initial fee to Knobs & Knockers is £7,000. The chain then charges a 7% turnover management service fee. Around £12,000 worth of opening stocks are required. The franchisor estimates the cost of shopfitting and display equipment will amount to around £21,000. There will be further working capital needs of around £15,000, adding up to a total start-up cost of £55,000. Of this around £35,000 could generally be financed from a clearing bank in the form of a £25,000 initial capital loan and a £10,000 overdraft for working capital. Hence any prospective franchisee will need £20,000 of his/her own funds to establish the franchise on a firm financial base.

How Profitable Is It?

Sales projections suggest turnover of £130,000 in year one rising to £200,000 by year three. At a gross profit margin of 51%, gross profits will be in the region of £88,000 by year three. In the sample projections Knobs & Knockers provide, they allow for depreciation of the shopfitting costs, amortisation of the lease premium and overdraft interest — items excluded from many franchisor projections. Nevertheless, profits before drawings and term loan repayments by year three can reach £25,000. It is important to bear in mind that as a business proprietor you can consider yourself 'self-employed' for taxation purposes, you will consequently be taxed under

Schedule D Case I. This allows you to write off allowable expenses againt gross profits, and can frequently be more tax efficient than being an employee.

Where Are The Opportunities?

Most of Knobs & Knockers retail operations are concentrated in the Home Counties or major urban areas such as Manchester or Leeds. There are very few in the North of England or Scotland and Wales, and few in the West; there are obviously opportunities in the Midlands, too. The advantage of many of these areas is that property costs will be significantly lower than in the Greater London area where Knobs & Knockers has most outlets. Consequently start-up costs and break-even point are more accessible for those with less money to invest in a franchise.

Further Information

If you wish to pursue this franchise, you should contact:

Franchise Director,
Knobs & Knockers Franchising Limited,
Hathaway House,
7D Woodfield Road,
London   W9 2EA

Telephone: 01-289 4764

Intacab

The Business

Intabcab is a franchised taxi service. The franchisee sets up with a fleet of around eleven cabs, using the smart yellow Intacab livery. These cabs are radio controlled from a central office. Business is obtained from both account and cash customers, who will, Intacab hope, choose a recognisable name against an unknown local service. Intacab help obtain various local authority licenses, site permissions, the selection of vehicles, technical training, computer analysis of operations and staff and driver selection and training. Intacab was started in Basildon in 1975 and modelled on the Chicago Yellow Cab Company in the USA. It commenced franchising in 1980.

The taxi trade is highly fragmented and fairly competitive. Although it is easy to set up in business as a minicab operator, it is a much harder task to run an efficient and profitable fleet of taxis. Traditionally the business has suffered from more than its fair share of cowboy independent operators, and many business and private users find it difficult to get good service − outside the well-organised black cab outfits working in the centres of cities.

But the profits can be attractive. Not only do people rely on taxis ever more − to avoid drink driving, having to park their car etc − it is a full seven days and nights a week trade in many areas. Consequently the assets are fully utilized, so the return ought to be high.

Hackney carriages are cash businesses which can

generate business without marketing spend thanks to their scarcity value. Private hire cars require marketing expenditure in order to get customers, since they cannot wait in taxi ranks or be hailed in traffic.

What Does Intacab Offer?

Intacab believe their trade mark and smart yellow livery carries value, and will become increasingly recognised by customers as the network of franchisees spreads across the country. Intacab help franchises to find and adapt a site to suit the operation of a taxi control centre. Intacab also help with the purchase and lease of vehicles; they suggest their purchasing power can obtain discounts on vehicles, spares, fuel and equipment. The same applies with the firm's radio control equipment. Franchisees are supplied with a complete system of documentation control, a complete accounting system and corporate stationery. A comprehensive marketing campaign is launched when the franchisee starts up, via advertising, direct mail shots, and leaflet distribution.

Computab supplies computerised control management systems to monitor driver and vehicle running costs. Each franchisee undertakes a very full training in all aspects of the business — legal, maintenance, personnel, marketing, control systems etc. Intacab also helps obtain the licences necessary, which may include hackney carriage licences, private hire vehicle licences, operators licences, and a home office licence for radio equipment.

What Does It Cost?

An initial £6,000 franchise fee is charged, and a goodwill payment of perhaps £15,000 is normally necessary to secure a second-hand hackney carriage licence.

This licence however retains its value and indeed may appreciate. Taximeters and radio equipment will cost perhaps £3,500. Decor to Intacab premises and office equipment, computer and telephone installation will cost around £14,500. Seven hire and reward cars will need advance finance payments of at least £6,000. There are working capital needs of perhaps £5,000 to cover sundry items such as an initial fuel stock. The total outlay adds up to £40,000. Up to half of this sum can be borrowed without security from the High Street banks. The net capital requirement on behalf of the franchisee will thus be between £20,000 and £25,000.

Intacab charge a levy of 7% on turnover. The licencee is expected to finance his own vehicles. Vehicles are written off over about three years. Intacab stress that the assets an Intacab franchisee accumulates are readily realisable in the open market, while many franchise operations invest in equipment that is useless outside the franchise.

What Profits Can I Make?

Assuming you have 20 vehicles in use by year three, your turnover might reach around £420,000. After driver costs, diesel, vehicle expenses, advertising and Intacab's royalty, the gross profit would amount to around £159,000. Further costs including vehicle depreciaton and lease charges, rent, rates and telephone would leave around £50,000 annual profits before interest, drawings and tax. As an operating margin of about 12.5% this seems about right.

This projection suggests each vehicle will complete 60,000 miles per annum and earn about 34p per mile revenue – excluding VAT. Vehicles are purchased on 24 month lease schemes.

How Do I Take It From Here?

You should contact:

Peter Dance,
Intacab Ltd.,
Service House,
West Mayne,
Basildon,
Essex.

Telephone: Basildon (0628) 415891

A mutually convenient preliminary meeting can be arranged.

Holiday Inns

The Business

The first Holiday Inn opened in Memphis in 1952. Since then over 1,600 hotels across 52 countries have opened, providing some 320,000 guest rooms. Nearly 90% of these hotels are operated through franchise agreements. Holiday Inn offers a world-famous brand name — possibly the best known in the hospitality business — operating systems, technology, advertising and marketing support, as well as staff training — plus significant feedback from market research programmes.

In 1988 Bass the UK brewer bought the rights to Holiday Inn outside the North American continent and they are actively expanding. The British lodging industry has boomed in recent years, thanks to increased business customer traffic and a roaring tourist trade. Our popularity as a spot for foreign visitors looks set to grow in the years to come, while ever more executive travel and such events as conferences and trade shows mean more good quality hotels will be needed. The field has a number of major groups competing ferociously, and plenty of smaller operators, but there are still gaps for newcomers to make their presence felt. And of course those already involved in the hotel business might wish to gain from the reputation and experience of Holiay Inn by becoming a franchisee.

In the USA most Holiday Inns have been built from scratch rather than emerging from a conversion. In Europe there is usually less space, so adapted older hotels have sometimes proved adequate. In either case, Holiday Inn will expect to see a property developed according to their specifications. When construction work is completed, Holiday Inn grant a licence for a minimum period of 20 years.

Holiday Inn now have three types of hotel. There is the standard hotel, with double bedrooms, sixteen hour room service, a swimming pool and leisure facilities, complemented by a variety of meeting and conference rooms. The Holiday Inn Crown Plaza concept is smarter and more expensive, aimed squarely at the business market rather than tourists. The third type of hotel is the Holiday Inn Garden Court, with quality but no-frills service and a reduced complement of common parts. These require a reduced level of capital investment, and given the space restrictions and costs, are the most likely route for most UK franchisees.

What Does It Cost?

The level of investment needed from the franchisor depends entirely on the particular project. The cost of constructing a Holiday Inn Garden Court hotel averages about £35,000 per room — ie a cost of £3.5 million for a 100 room hotel. The franchisee will generally supply an equity investment of between 25% and 40% of the anticipated cost, with land costs accounting for no more than 20%. Obviously few individuals have say £1.5 million unencumbered capital. Frequently consortia are formed to pool resources and jointly invest. A typical number of participants might be twelve, each contributing say £150,000 — rather like an ad hoc Lloyds insurance syndicate. Probably at least one of the investors will have catering and hotel trade experience, and will lead the management of the hotel. Franchise fees fall into two categories: (i) an initial application fee, followed by a royalty based on a percentage of revenue; and (ii) fixed payments into common funds to cover the cost of marketing, advertising and system reservation services. The size of these fees and royalties depend upon the scale of the operation, but might average 5% royalty, £25,000 initial fee, and £15,000 annual contribution to advertising.

What Do I Get?

Holiday Inn helps supervise the construction of the hotel according to exacting standards, after they have satisfied themselves through a feasibility study that the site has potential. They sign an agreement with a franchisee for a minimum period of 20 years or 12 years for a Holiday Inn Garden Court hotel.

Holiday Inns benefit directly from continuous product development, market research, advertising and promotional campaigns both worldwide and within each region. Over $50 million is spent annually on advertising and PR, with 4,200 sales people promoting the benefits of Holiday Inns to key customers and corporate and travel accounts. There is also the massive International Central Reservations Office network, which books 30 million roomnights a year through 1,100 reservation agents. The system is linked to five of the largest airline reservation systems, giving immediate access from 150,000 terminals in travel agents and airline offices. This network is the most powerful contributor to hotel occupancy in the world.

Holiday Inn offer franchisees one of the finest training programmes in the world for their staff. They also provide administration, catering, personnel, recruitment and leisure facilities management systems.

What Profits Can I Make?

A 100 bed Holiday Inn should turn over at least £2 million annually once fully established. Overall net profits can be of the order of £300,000 before depreciation, tax and interest costs. The hotel business has proved highly profitable in recent years in terms of both income generated and the rise in capital values in hotels. In central locations like London, hotel values have risen by at least 20% per annum for some years — despite the volatility of the tourist trade. Consequently a major investment such as required to build a Holiday Inn should be seen giving a return both in terms of the capital worth of the business, and the profit stream generated by its operation.

What Should I Do Next?

For a modestly informative brochure contact Holiday Inn and upon receipt of details of a hotel project from you, talks will progress. Their address is:

Holiday Inns International,
Administrative Office,
62 London Road,
Staines,
Middlesex   TW18 4JE

Telephone: (0784) 66266

Fast Frame

The Business

Fast Frame is probably the best known of a new breed of High Street shops which specialise in rapid picture framing. It has been developed in the last few years specifically as a franchise concept. It combines traditional skills with the latest in framing technology to give a smart finish at reasonable prices with a very rapid turnaround. A wide range of framing is undertaken, including oil paintings, lithography, screen work, photographs, tapestries, water colours, certificates etc. Over 100 different mouldings are held in stock and a simple, efficient pricing system enables speedy handling of customers' requirements. The profit margins are excellent, since the materials costs are low, the labour content minimal, but value added is high.

In recent years the numbers of pictures and designs properly framed for exhibition in the home has soared. Ordinary people have taken to putting up smart posters, prints and paintings in their homes. Fast Frame, along with one or two others, offers a cheaper and quicker method of framing than the old-fashioned back street outlet. The shops are well-located, bright and clean and staff are helpful and service rapid.

What You Get

Fast Frame will help you choose a site and negotiate lease and planning details. They conduct a thorough survey of the area before you sign up to ensure the location will provide sufficient customer traffic. The design team of

Fast Frame draw up a full shopfitting specification and internal layout plan. You are supplied with the framing equipment and tools necessary to run the shop. All the office equipment and furniture is provided. A full training programme is undertaken by each franchisee and there are staff training programmes available too. By the end of this course, you are proficient in the various framing techniques and in offering customers advice about the range of frames available and colour combinations and such matters as mounts, stretching tapestries, conservation framing, when to use non-reflective glass etc. Fast Frame supervise the store fitting-out to ensure it is an efficient work space while still being attractive to customers. A full launch is undertaken to introduce Fast Frame to the local business, commercial and consumer communities. An ongoing series of advertising, promotional, and point-of-sale materials and activities are organised by Fast Frame to bring custom to the new branch's door.

What It Costs

The initial Fast Frame package comes with a fairly high price tag of £34,000 plus VAT, but this does give you a fully finished shop ready to trade. Of course, in addition you will need initial finance for working capital of perhaps £4,000. However, initial stock is paid for over 6 months by 6 interest free payments built into trading cash flow. There may well be other costs such as a retained agent securing the property, or a premium payable on a lease. The royalty/management fee charged is 6 and a quarter percent of turnover, with a further 6 and a quarter percent to cover all marketing costs. But Fast Frame do allow you to pay for initial stock over 6 months through 6 interest free payments, which should be fundable through cash-flow. Fast Frame suggest that up to two-thirds of the total capital requirement can be funded through one of the major bank's franchisee schemes, without necessarily having additional security for these borrowings.

How Profitable Is It?

While initial turnover is projected to be £60,000, illustrations suggest a turnover of £150,000 can be achieved by year four. The net profit before depreciation, tax, drawings and finance cost on £150,000 would be £37,700. This assumes an outlet with a fairly full rent, rates and insurance bill of £35,000 which would secure an excellent site in most towns. These costs include wages and National Insurance of over £17,000 a year at a turnover of £150,000. This figure can obviously be reduced if a husband and wife team are tackling the franchise together.

Overall Fast Frame offers potential franchisees fairly typical projected profits in a successful location, and shows what a high margin this business is: 25% at the net level!

How To Take It Further

To receive the Fast Frame franchise brochure you should write to their head office:

Fast Frame,
28 Blandford Street
Sunderland   SR1 3JH.

Telephone: (091) 565 2233

Exchange Travel

What Is It?

Exchange Travel is the only truly successful franchised retail travel agency. It numbers over 50 franchised units and has become a well-known brand name on the High Street since it started franchising in 1984. It offers both consumer and business travel services, while the holding company operates a separate tour arm.

The foreign holiday market has grown consistently for a number of years at a rate in excess of 8% compound. Most leisure analysts predict this trend will continue, as more people buy package holidays abroad. Travel agents have grown in tandem with this marketplace by supplying products from airlines, tour operators, shipping companies etc. In addition, business travel has expanded, and travel agents have carved out a profitable niche in this area in recent years.

Exchange Travel has two strong selling points. Firstly, it offers branch membership of ABTA — the Association of British Travel Agents — which is a necessary qualification in order to avoid being a 'bucket shop' agency. Normally gaining membership of ABTA is a lengthy process and rarely a certainty. Secondly, thanks to its buying clout and size, Exchange Travel can arrange average commissions of about 12% — far higher than the typical independent travel agent's 8% commission rate.

Travel agency is a highly competitive business, and trying to match rivals in price means margins can be uncomfortably tight. Exchange Travel's credibility attracts customers who want a reliable supplier. Such customers may well be willing to pay more for the extra security of dealing with an established name. Exchange Travel markets widely, and this recognition among the public draws trade from both corporate accounts and holidaymakers. Travel agencies enjoy high turnover, since they deal in expensive items – people's holidays – but the net margins are usually under 10% of sales. However, interest can be earned on holiday deposit money etc – so there are benefits to generating such a high turnover.

What Does It Cost

An Exchange Travel franchise is not cheap. Exchange Travel charge a one-off initial fee of £7,500 plus VAT, and a higher than average 12% of revenue (equating to about 1% of sales). Moreover franchisees are expected to contribute 5% of revenue towards the Marketing Services Fund. This sum is fully expended and audited on behalf of the franchisee. The franchisor recommends start-up franchisees contribute a minimum of £25,000 equity and a Director's loan of between £5,000 and £35,000 depending upon the size of the site. Additionally a bank overdraft of up to £65,000 at its peak will need to be negotiated. Exchange Travel offer an unusual guarantee in that they will buy back the franchise branch at any time for a minimum valuation of 7.5% of the previous twelve months' turnover.

Exchange Travel estimate the shopfitting and office capital equipment costs at around £35,000 for a medium sized branch. Profits should be generated in year three, with potentially above average profits for the travel trade by year four. By year seven Exchange Travel suggests a franchisee should have a business investment which has provided a return and which has a worth of between £250,000 and £440,000, depending upon turnover. A cumulative average return estimated at 35% per annum should be achieved over the period of the first seven year contract.

What Profits Can Be Achieved?

An Exchange Travel branch in a local shopping centre should turn over around £1.5 million by year six, allowing for a 5% annual rate of inflation. This will generate revenues at 12% of sales of over £180,000. After total costs and overheads of £150,000, the net profit should be at least £30,000. For a branch in an area shopping centre a £40,000 pretax profit by year six should be a realistic target; for a regional shopping centre £50,000 pretax profit should be taken as a target.

How Do I Take It From Here?

Contact the Franchise Development Department at
Exchange Travel Agency Limited,
Exchange House,
Parker Road,
East Sussex TN34 3UB.

Telephone: (0424) 423571

Crown Eyeglass

The Business

Crown is one of the major groups of shops selling spectacles in competition with opticians. Following a change in the law in December 1984, it became legal for non-qualified opticians to sell glasses. Now glasses can be sold like other High Street goods and there are opportunities for consumers to shop around and get better value. Crown is the largest optical franchise operation in the UK. They sell spectacles on prescription for as little as £9.95 a pair, as against perhaps as much as £80 a pair from an opthalmic optician. Crown franchisees cannot dispense prescriptions, but they still address a substantial market. Over 60% of all adults wear spectacles, and many people are now choosing to own more than one pair of glasses — whether for convenience in case of breakage, or for fashion reasons. Meanwhile the public are realising that equal quality spectacles costing 70% less are available from such retail centres as Crown units.

Over 11 million people have their eyes tested every year and three in four are prescribed glasses — hence over 8 million pairs are sold every year, and the numbers continue to rise. Crown works by supplying lense prescriptions to order after franchisees help customers choose a pair of frames. Crown has a purpose built factory for dispensing glasses.

Crown's franchise seems primarily aimed at those wanting to run a small unit as an add-on in a bigger store, or possibly in a location like an indoor market hall. Little space is needed, since minimal stock need be carried.

How Much Does It Cost?

The up-front payment to Crown for a franchise is quite steep — £20,000 plus VAT. This does however safeguard the franchisee's exclusive selling rights to Crown products in an agreed area for five years. There is then an option to renew the agreement at no further cost. There is effectively no ongoing royalty payment. Instead franchisees agreed to buy from Crown their spectacles and frames. Crown clearly enjoy a trade mark-up on such sales. Crown say they subsidise local advertising costs from time to time by 50%, but other local marketing expenditure will have to be undertaken by the franchisee. Crown operate a stock rotation system whereby they accept return of certain slow-selling items.

What Do You Get?

Crown offer to fit out your shop. They are somewhat unspecific about their contribution, which presumably varies depending upon whether it is a stall-type outlet or a stand-alone branch. Crown promise to provide franchisees with the latest technical equipment and a full training. All the necessary patient record material is supplied, along with accounting books etc. You are also provided with 400 assorted frames, and the Jewel Collection of frames.

What Profits Can You Make?

Opticians have traditionally made most of their profits from selling spectacles and contact lenses — normally at huge mark-ups. Now it is possible to participate in this large and lucrative market without spending many years acquiring an opthalmic optician's qualification Crown offers a convenient route. It makes and supplies competitive frames and prepares prescriptions economically. This allows you to offer fine products at cheaper prices than most of your rivals — and still make a good margin.

Crown suggest their more successful franchisees are making gross profits of over £700 a week, which might indicate a pretax profit of perhaps £20,000 a year, depending upon overheads. This compares favourably with a number of other retail franchises. However, the heavy upfront bias of the 'cost' of the franchise is something of a negative, since it gives less incentive to the franchisor to see the franchisee make high sales — and profits!

Where To Go From Here

If you're interested in becoming a Crown franchisee, you should call Crown on (0254) 51535 and ask for a brochure, or write to:

Joe Lee,
Managing Director,
Crown Eyeglass plc,
Stancliffe Street,
Blackburn   BB2 2QR

ComputerLand

The Business

ComputerLand is a major US public company and the largest computing franchising network in the world. It was founded in 1976 in California and now numbers over 750 centres across the US and 23 other countries around the rest of the world. Its European operations commenced in Brussels in 1978 — there are now over 100 centres dotted right across the EEC, and 20 in Britain.

ComputerLand is a microcomputer hardware and software supplier. It offers full service personal computing products from retail outlets, dealing in major brand name products, primarily servicing the business community. It emphasises its unbiased advice, training and on-going technical support which it provides to customers.

The computer industry has grown since World War II into one of the largest commercial undertakings in the West. Most projections suggest computers will continue to become ever more important. The advent of the personal computer in the 1970s revolutionised the computing industry and has led to massive office automation. But there is a proliferation of confusing and constantly changing products available and a large degree of technical ignorance of computers among users. Systems suppliers, who sell computers, peripherals, networks and software packages, have grown up to help users choose and understand a mix of machines and programmes which solve their problems. The ever-continuing and exponential growth in PC usage and sales have proved a fertile market for service-oriented suppliers like ComputerLand, who offer independent and tailor-made solutions.

What Do You Get?

ComputerLand has a strong brand name which is recognised in most places and is of particular use in a field like professional computing supplies and services, where customers want reliability and credibility above all else. ComputerLand help franchisees locate and secure sites and use their research skills to determine whether a given unit has enough customer traffic, parking etc to succeed. They will help franchisees fit out and design the store so as to maximise sales and product exposure, and maintain the group's powerful corporate identity. ComputerLand provide a wealth of sales literature and a full training programme for all franchisees, to ensure they reach customers and are able to help them. Franchisees are also given instruction in administration and accounting procedures, in order to keep tight financial controls on the business. ComputerLand keep substantial stocks of all equipment available for franchisees, bought on favourable terms using Computer-Land's bulk purchasing power. ComputerLand vets all products and selects only those appropriate for its markets, and receives many products before the competition direct from manufacturers. It also receives top rate service from product suppliers, who know how important it is as a customer.

What Is The Cost?

ComputerLand is one of the more expensive franchises available. A centre for a medium sized market in an area of up to 1,000,000 inhabitants will require a total investment of between £300,000 and £360,000. Of this £20,000 is the initial franchise fee and £70,000 goes towards initial inventory, inclduing demo equipment. Leasehold improvements will cost around £50,000, while fixtures will cost around £35,000. Furniture and equipment will cost a further £40,000. There is a £45,000 approx working capital requirement. Training, legal, accounting and insurance costs swallow another £45,000. A property premium might well be payable in addition to the above sums. ComputerLand charge a 3.5% gross royalty on sales. Franchisees must also contribute 1% of gross monthly sales to the advertising and marketing fund to use nationally. The franchise agreement lasts for ten years, with the opportunity to renew for a further ten years by mutual agreement.

What Profits Can You Make?

ComputerLand do not publish projected sales and profit figures, but a capable franchisee should expect to turn over at least £700,000 in a successful outlet and make pre-tax and drawings profits of between £75,000 and £100,000. Selling computer equipment and providing training, support and maintenance services is a highly profitable business if successful.

If You Want Further Information

Contact ComputerLand and they will provide a brochure:

ComputerLand Europe SA,
UK Regional Office,
518 Elder House,
Elder Gate,
Central Milton Keynes   MK9 1LR.

Telephone: (0908) 664244

Clarks Shoe Shops

What Is The Business?

Clarks is one of the best known high street retailers of shoes — it ranks about second in the UK, with over 500 outlets. It has been franchising shops since 1965 and has over 150 franchised outlets. While the footwear retailing trade is competitive and seeing minimal growth, Clarks is a respected brand name and their retailers make better margins than most, partly thanks to their rather up-market image. Torlink is the C & J Clark Ltd subsidiary which deals with the independent retailers. It receives offers of new sites in shopping centres which Clarks' take on lease and then sub-let to the independent owner.

The shoe shop sells Clarks, K Shoes and Levis for Feet brands. The brand limitation increases profitability through manufacturers' high volume rebates, better stockturn and reduced markdowns. Clarks arrange a guaranteed loan to help fund the business in most cases; these are available on very competitive terms from the leading clearing banks. Their designers offer a subsidised design and shopfitting service specialising in shoe shop modelling. At least part of this is arranged on interest-free credit. A full training programme is undertaken, including a week of classroom lessons and period of retail experience. On an ongoing basis, once the business is up and running, a consultant will offer subsidised advice. You don't pay any advertising levy, despite the fact that through television, posters and the press, Clarks is easily the most heavily promoted shoe brand. Your shop will be kept provided with all the latest point-of-sale and display material. You'll also benefit from Clarks' considerable expertise with computer systems to give you maximum control over stock and cash.

The footwear retailing trade is a highly competitive one, with Sears (BSC) dominating the market with a 30% plus share. The numbers of pairs of shoes bought annually is not rising, but their cost is, so the value of the market has climbed. However, some observers feel the market is over supplied with shops, and many outlets owned by major chains make poor returns. The trade is characterised by high stock costs, in order to be able to supply a shoe to fit, and a highly seasonal trading pattern, with most of the profit generated during the winter months. Clarks outlets are at the top end of the market and charge premium prices. If the success of retailers like Next, who are new to shoes but seem to be doing well, is any indication, then Clarks shops occupy a profitable niche.

What Does It Cost?

Clarks/Torlink offer a remarkably generous package. They require you as franchisee to stump up at least £25,000. Of this, the start up fee is a fairly modest £10,200, which includes all site-finding fees, installation of an EPOS computer system and the various costs such as solicitors', landlords' and agents' fees, land registry, stamp duty, limited company formation, and arrangement of a guaranteed loan. Thanks to Clarks shopfit loan, the only bank facility required is around £25,000, which should be cheaper than you would otherwise be able to obtain, thanks to Clarks' guarantee. Of the £80,000 initial funding, almost half goes towards design and shopfitting; around 40% goes towards stock (the cost of which is relatively high and unavoidably so in the shoe trade, since a range of styles and sizes must be stocked in depth to remain competitive). Clarks offer an interest-free shopfit loan on a proportion of the total shopfit cost; this loan is repayable over 5 years in 10 equal half-yearly instalments. Bank loans are repayable in equal instalments

101

over a period of 5 years, commencing at the beginning of the second trading year.

What Profits Can I Make?

Gross sales in a unit of 100 square metres should be around £200,000 including VAT. The gross profit margin is about 40%. Assuming rent, rates, electricity, wages and NI, promotional costs and administration charges of about £26,000, the trading surplus generated should be of the order of £25,000. Clarks then allow for directors' drawings of £11,500, giving a net profit before interest, tax and capital repayments — but after shopfit/lease depreciation — of £10,000 in year one. This rises to £12,000 by year two. The projected profits seem modest compared with many other franchisors, but I think Clarks are being far more honest in their figures about the true costs. If a successful outlet is established then growth from £200,000 sales should be achieved, to generate a higher net profit.

Further Information

Clarks offer a fairly generous package by most franchisor standards, and they are choosy about who they select as franchisees. You will be required to complete a pretty detailed application form, giving details of previous employment and education, your financial resources, and references. To receive one of these forms and a brochure, contact:

Torlink Ltd.,
Box 106,
40 High Street,
Street,
Somerset,
BA16 OYA.

Telephone: Street (0458) 43131

Burger King

What Is It?

Burger King is the world's second largest fast food hamburger restaurant chain, after McDonalds. It now has more than 5,000 outlets, over 500 outside the US across 26 countries. Average annual restaurant sales are significantly above $1 million. It has 18 restaurants in the UK, with five of them free-standing drive-thru restaurants. It plans up to 225 franchised restaurants in the UK and is actively recruiting in London and the south-east.

Burger King is yet another beneficiary of the increasing trend towards eating-out, helped by the growth in car ownership, women working and disposable incomes. The UK has relatively few of the major hamburger chains — Wimpy being the only domestic competitor of size. McDonalds has been a major success, but has expanded mainly by company-owned outlets. Burger King clearly aims to emulate their considerable success in this country.

In the US Burger King works with major corporations in providing hamburger facilities — Greyhound, Woolworth and many colleges are examples. There are also instances of multiple franchisees of Burger King. These are individuals or partnerships who operate more than one franchise outlet. Few franchises have reached such critical mass in the UK yet, but the time is soon coming when multiple franchisees will be common.

Burger King outlets enjoy high turnovers and healthy margins. The capital costs to establish a restaurant are considerable, but the ongoing investment required is minimal, and the payback period normally less than five years. The return on investment should exceed 20% by the third year of operations.

How Much Does It Cost?

Burger King expects franchisees to have net worth of at least £500,000, and liquid assets (cash, shares, bonds etc) of around half this amount. The total development cost of a typical site is between £600,000 and £700,000 – and this excludes the property purchase or lease premium element. Burger King charge a 4% royalty on sales, and expect a 4% commission towards overall marketing costs. There is also a £17,000 one-off fee to commence. Hamburger take-aways spend heavily on all forms of advertising and sponsorship, and stage substantial promotions frequently.

The Royal Bank of Scotland in conjunction with Burger King will offer up to 70% of the total start-up financial requirement by way of loan and/or overdraft. The maximum period of the loan is 10 years; a capital repayment holiday is available for the first 12 months. Interest is charged at 2% to 4% over base rates, with a 1% arrangement fee. Personal assets in addition to the assets of the business may be needed as security.

Depending on whether an in-line or drive-thru store is operated, operating profits should be between 17% and 21% of turnover. Assuming sales exceed £500,000, operating profits should therefore be around £100,000 per annum. This figure is before the 4% royalty deduction and tax and the cost of funds employed – including interest on borrowed money. Of course, there should be considerable uplift in the value of the restaurant once it is turning over £0.5 million. Frequently restaurants can change hands for as much as two and a half times annual sales – for leasehold sites!

What Do You Get?

Burger King is a well-known brand name in parts of Great

Britain, despite the presence of only 20 sites. The franchisor has a wealth of experience in setting up fast-food outlets. Burger King has developed a whole range of systems and suppliers, from staff recruitment procedures to computerised till systems to cooking methods which ensure the public gets good food and the restaurant makes a suitable profit. Burger King can help identify and procure a location for the franchisee, although they will not take a financial interest in the property. The franchisor understands how to construct a cost-effective establishment, and obtain the relevant consents and approvals from various authorities. Burger King has developed a range of suppliers who provide the finest products at competitive prices. The restaurant chain is in addition constantly developing new menu ideas to keep customers coming through the doors.

All franchisee teams should appoint an operating partner who will attend a 12-week intensive training programme to become familiar with all operational aspects of running a Burger King restaurant. The minimum development timescale for a restaurant is 4 months. But the Burger King agreement is in force for 20 years, and can be assigned (with Burger King's approval) to a buyer.

What Profits Can You Make?

An in-line West End outlet of say 4,000 sq ft should generate perhaps £500,000 of sales annually. Total food costs will be around £140,000, with wage etc costs of perhaps £90,000, leaving an overall operating profit of £270,000. Further overheads including light, heat etc, advertising, rent, depreciation and interest will amount to £145,000. Other sales and controllable expenses will be about £40,000. Thus the pretax, before loan repayment net profit should be about £85,000. This represents a margin on sales of around 17%, which demonstrates just what a profitable business a fast-food restaurant can be. A freestanding operation can make an even more impressive 21% margin, suggesting profits of over £100,000 on a £500,000 annual turnover.

What Do You Do Next?

You should write to:

Burger King (UK) Ltd.,
Franchising Department,
20 Kew Road,
Richmond,
Surrey TW9 2NA.

Telephone: 01-940 6046

Avis Car Rental

The Business

Avis is the largest car rental company in Europe, Africa, and the Middle East, though it ranks behind Hertz in the US. From its beginnings in Detroit, it has expanded to a world-wide fleet of over 250,000 vehicles across 3,500 offices. Short-term car rental is still a growth business in Britain, despite fierce competition from the likes of Budget and National. While Avis founded its success on rental from airport locations, the next stage of growth is likely to be from urban and in-town sites. Customers who patronise these type of operations include local firms needing extra transportation during peak times, individuals needing cars for special occasions, and insured persons who need a temporary replacement car after an accident or breakdown. Corporate and tourist users comprise a large proportion of the business base. This is a business which requires a reasonable amount of capital, since both premises and vehicles are needed — although the latter can be leased. Many prosperous operators have converted old filling stations or garages into rental units with great success.

Avis have over 50 company owned rental car sites in the UK and over 50 franchisee operations. They plan to more than double the number of franchise outlets to 120 over a period of years.

What You Get And What It Takes

Avis do offer a powerful brand name and image in the marketplace, enshrined with their legendary 'We Try

Harder' advertising slogan. They buy fleet cars in sufficient quantities to be able to negotiate significant economies of scale with the major vehicle manufacturers under bulk purchasing arrangements – as a licensee you will benefit from these savings. Avis also negotiate very favourable fleet insurance rates. Avis offer their licensees expert advice, training and business systems such as billing and account records. Licensees are included in the Avis worldwide directory and the Yellow Pages under Avis' large advert. Avis undertake major advertising campaigns and marketing intitiatives, and supply brochures, point of sale material and uniforms. Licensees also get business from the 5 million strong customer base of Avis card holders worldwide, and the Avis Wizard computerised reservation system. Each licensee has a protected and exclusive area. Avis may be able to help with securing premises in certain cases.

What Does It Cost?

Licensees meanwhile are expected to advertise locally, and to participate in the various Avis services offered such as one-way rental systems. Avis licensees must pay an initial licence fee which depends on the market size, and 10% of revenue – a fairly high royalty rate for a franchise deal. Avis accounting and documentation systems must be adopted and minimum standards adhered to throughout the rental operation. Prospective licensees are expected to invest a minimum of £50,000 initially, and possess sufficient collateral to secure loans necessary for the vehicle and working capital requirements of the business. An initial licence fee is also payable, dependent upon available market size; a typical urban area might cost a minimum of £10,000 as a one-off payment to Avis. The franchisee must operate a yearly average vehicle fleet mutually agreed between Avis and the franchisee. The licence meanwhile cannot be transferred without approval from Avis. Avis are a highly experienced franchisee group and therefore know what to expect of decent franchisees. There are a number of programmes such as the one-way rental system which franchisees must agree to participate in; franchisees should honour the various Avis charge cards and make sure all rentals are filled out using the comprehensive Avis documentation systems.

More Information

For further details on franchise opportunities with Avis, you should write to the:

> Franchise Manager,
> Avis Rent A Car Ltd.,
> Trident House,
> Station Road,
> Hayes,
> Middlesex   UB3 4DJ.

Athena

The Business

Athena is a well-known High Street retailer of prints, posters, cards and stationery. There are over 60 of these high profile outlets run by Pentos, the holding company, in the UK, and further branches in the US and Europe. Athena now produces a wide range of its own posters, postcards and greetings cards with special appeal to the teens and twenties age group which comprise its main customer base. Recently Athena outlets have begun to stock books, framed pictures, and gifts. It probably has the strongest and most fashionable brand name in this highly fragmented business. Pentos, owning Dillons, Athena (both the shops and card supplier), and Ryman, is easily the largest in this specialist paper-products field, and achieves significant distribution and scale purchasing economies for its franchisees. The margins available on such items as posters, giftwrap, greetings cards and stationery are excellent — as high as 100% in many cases. The significant resource of constantly changing Athena-designed products mean Athena franchises are ahead of most of the competition. Sales of such items as cards are still growing among the under 25 age bracket (to which Athena has particular appeal), and women buy over 75% of all such goods. Athena is strongly represented in the South-East, but many towns in the Midlands and North do not have a branch.

What You Get And What It Costs

Once you sign up as an Athena franchisee, the

franchisor's professional property arm will evalute suitable premises, negotiate the lease and if necessary use Pentos' good covenant to secure the title. A complete design and shopfitting service will undertake the elaborate interior and smart fascia. You will then undergo up to seven weeks training both at the Athena head office and at an established Athena unit. You will receive the Athena Franchise Owners' Handbook and Operating Manual, which give you advice on stock, merchandising, and accounting systems. You will be entitled to advantageous purchasing terms, backed by substantial group discount terms. The burden of monthly sales and costs analysis, PAYE calculations, together with VAT returns and draft annual trading accounts preparation is taken care of by the franchisor. This permits the owner to run the outlet to its maximum, while being in total possession of all the relevant management accounting information to keep control of the business.

The initial licence fee payable to Athena is £7,500. The typical costs of shopfitting and interior are around £50,000. Lease premiums are payable in half of all outlets − normally reflecting below market rental. In addition professional fees and expenses when negotiating the lease might be as much as £5,000, while working capital of at least £10,000 should be allowed for advance rent, rate, insurance etc costs. The initial stock order will be granted on a 90 day credit facility, so that stock payment should be covered by cash flow. As in any business of reasonable size, provision has to be made on the franchise package payments for VAT at 15% − around £9,400 in this case. The total costs might therefore come to £82,000.

Athena will prepare on behalf of franchisees a comprehensive dossier of financial data for bank presentation purposes, in order to help obtain finance. Some clearing banks will provide 70% of the total funding requirement for respectable franchise operations like Athena. A typical package might consist of a 7 year term loan at say 3% over LIBOR, with an overdraft facility to provide working capital. A 1½ to 1% arrangement fee is payable to the bank and life cover for the amount of the loan will be required. The franchisee might be expected to stump up anything from £25,000 in cash as his contribution, depending upon circumstances.

Making It Work

Athena provide some quite impressive sample projections as to the trading levels which can be achieved. In a substantial unit you should do turnover of around £170,000 a year, which generates a pre-tax trading profit of over £30,000 a year, assuming a rent of £35,000 and a gross profit margin of 60%. Athena keep franchisees in touch regarding future product development, group merchandising, and sales trends and forecasts. An integrated accounting service is operated by Athena for all franchise owners. They take care of monthly sales and cost analysis, PAYE calculations, VAT returns and draft annual trading accounts. Franchisees must pay 1.5% of sales turnover each month for this service. Athena suggest that suppliers provide the chain with impressive discounts on goods they are able to order in bulk — up to 20%.

Athena outlets stock a wide variety of merchandise, much of which is exclusive to them and new on the marketplace. Pentos sources and tests its range of items from DIY picture frames to this year's poster, in an effort to provide its shops with items that really move off the shelves. In this way a franchisee is offered a better-selling stock mix than if an attempt was made to operate independently. Athena the franchisor also knows how to display a store's goods to ensure the higher-margin and best-selling items get sufficient prominence, and to ensure the public are drawn into the store.

How To Take It Further

Athena represents one of the most successful shop

formats available to franchisees. If you wish to know more, write for their detailed brochure:

Athena,
Berwick House,
35 Livery Street,
Birmingham B3 2BP.

Telephone: 021-236 6886

AlphaGraphics

The Business

This firm calls itself Printshops Of The Future. They are included despite having only just established them-selves in the UK, because I believe they offer excellent prospects. They are a rival to other retail instant print franchisors such as Pip, Kall Kwik and Prontaprint, but they serve customers with a number of novel features. They have in-house desktop publishing, electronic com-position and design, laser typesetting and an electronics communications system. They are using some of the latest print/transmission technology to give customers printed material quicker and cheaper than traditional methods. They continue to provide the more conven-tional facilities such as photocopying, offset printing and binding. They are firmly aimed at the business market, who want smart, economically prepared documents in double-quick time.

They occupy a broadly similar marketplace to Pip, and so the comments regarding its size and growth are equally applicable to both franchises. AlpahaGraphics with its innovative services is also at the leading edge. Customers who can use DTP systems can hire the in-house equipment by the hour. Customers can also arrange sophisticated link-ups via AlphaLink to elec-tronically transfer originals to the printshop. I have a strong feeling AlphaGraphics shops will be highly successful, and any franchisee starting now will be getting in on the ground floor.

In the US AlphaGraphics operate over 250 outlets, the vast majority of them franchised, after starting in

Arizona in 1970. The concept has worked well there, and Pindar, the UK master licensee, is confident that the pattern will be repeated here.

What Does It Cost?

AlphaGraphics costs more than a typical UK instant print shop. The franchisee will be expected to stump up an initial £50,000, and to borrow around £100,000. The initial franchisee fee is a hefty £19,000 − of which AlphaGraphics 'lend' you 50% or £9,500. The equipment package is expensive at £85,000, owing to the high-tech nature of the hardware, with £49,000 spent on reprographic plant alone. Property costs are estimated at £30,500, including a £23,000 fitting out cost. Stocks are around £3,500, and AlphaGraphics suggest a £20,000 contingency reserve for ongoing initial working capital requirements. AlphaGraphics do not reveal their royalty fee to outsiders, but you can expect it to be at least 5%, together with the further minimum 2% of sales going towards the advertising fund for the entire franchise.

What Do You Get?

AlphaGraphics as a matter of policy acquires properties on behalf of franchisees and arranges a sub-let. This removes worries about a franchisee being unable to provide the landlord with suitable convenant and guarantees, or being unable to pay a substantial premium. In some cases the rent will actually be lower, thanks to AlphaGraphic's parent's covenant. AlphaGraphics arranges all store design, alterations and fitting out. It employs specialist architectural and design consultants and shopfitters on a national basis, so permitting economy in costs and uniformly high standards. AlphaGraphics selects the very finest and most appropriate equipment, and negotiates for the benefit of franchisees, national contracts at most favourable prices. The new store owners train in the USA at the Tucson, Arizona AlphaGraphics school for three weeks, with a mixture of classroom theory and hands-on work. There is a further week of training in an existing UK store.

On a continuing basis AlphaGraphics provide a high level of accounts and administration support. Franchisees are linked via a specialist electronic communications system AlphaLink to the accounting format named AlphaAccount which centrally records the progress of each order. The AlphaGraphics purchasing power is important in achieving bulk economies for supplies like paper and ink. The AlphaGraphics manuals are invaluable guides to all the possible problems faced and ways of coping with them. There is also a Central Hotline for newer owners who are having difficulty with say their LazerGraphics system.

What Profits Can You Make?

AlphaGraphics do not give out projections as to the performance of their stores. You can expect to turn over in excess of £200,000 annually if the outlet is to be successful. You should make a net margin before drawings etc of at least 10% on those sales. This margin will climb with increasing sales, thanks to the relatively high fixed cost element in the business.

What Should You Do Next?

If you wish to pursue this franchise opportunity, you should write to:

AlphaGraphics Printshops Of The Future (UK) Ltd.,
Ryedale Building,
58/60 Piccadilly,
York Y01 1NX.

Telephone: (0904) 611344

ALSO AVAILABLE FROM ROSTERS

TALKING TURKEY by Alison Rice (£5.95)

A lively and entertaining look at this newest holiday sensation. Travel writer and broadcaster Alison Rice has produced an up-to-date guide to the main Turkish resorts and Istanbul. Aimed at visitors new to Turkey it explains what to see, where to stay — and equally important, what to avoid. Includes basic Turkish phrases plus hints on making the best of the food, wine and shopping available.

VIVA ESPANA by Edmund Swinglehurst (£5.95)

Discover the real Spain before the bulldozers and industrialists have destroyed its natural beauty. In this comprehensive guide to Spain, Edmund Swinglehurst, travel expert and author, has provided a fascinating glimpse behind the veil of Spain to show you the heart of the countryside, its people, its culture and its way of life.

CHAMPAGNE ON A BUDGET by Patrick Delaforce (£5.95)

Champagne is probably the world's most famous wine — yet few people have discovered the sparkling region where it is produced. Wine expert and travel writer Patrick Delaforce shows you how to enjoy a trip to the Champagne region, suggests tours, visits to vineyards and gives advice on the wines worth sampling. Aimed at the independent traveller who does not wish to bust his budget this book includes lists of medium priced hotels and restaurants plus handy hints on enjoying your stay.

FRENCH RIVIERA ON A BUDGET by Patrick Delaforce (£5.95)

The land of celebrities, champagne cocktails and caviare is just waiting to be discovered. In this timely guide travel writer Patrick Delaforce shows that you don't need to break the Bank at Monte Carlo to enjoy a stay among the rich and

famous along the world's famous Cote d'Azur. He lists medium priced hotels, restaurants plus plenty of advice on how to spend those sun filled days and fun filled nights.

BURGUNDY AND BEAUJOLAIS ON A BUDGET by Patrick Delaforce (£5.95)

Discover one of France's most beautiful wine regions without spending a fortune. Patrick Delaforce, wine expert and travel writer, reveals the true heart of the French countryside. Just one hour's drive from Paris lies Burgundy, famous the world over for its wines, but also one of the most beautiful and intriguing regions in France. For the gourmet there is the chance to visit the vineyards where Chablis and Beaujolais are made and sample local produce such as truffles, river fish, fine game and fresh fruits. Includes: regional tours, local wines and wine co-operatives, value for money accommodation and restaurants, places of interest, regional events.

GASCONY AND ARMAGNAC ON A BUDGET by Patrick Delaforce (£5.95)

Discover one of France's best kept secrets — the land of brandy, beaches and Basque cuisine. Wine expert and travel writer Patrick Delaforce reveals the heart of one of France's most inviting holiday locations. From the beautiful silver coast fringed with pine forests through to the inland villages, there is an alluring countryside just waiting to be discovered. Magnificent beaches, sophisticated nightlife and superb cuisine. Includes: regional tours, local wines and wine co-operatives, value for money hotels and restaurants, places of interest and regional events.

IS IT WORTH ANYTHING? by Stephen Ellis (£3.99)

Most of us have drawers filled with odds and ends. But are they worth anything? Stephen Ellis writes on the money pages of the Daily Mirror which gets thousands of letters from readers asking just that. So here for everyone who cannot

bear to throw anything away 'just in case' is the book which will give most of the answers. Includes: toys, stamps, glass, jewellery, postcards, records and much more.

COOK AND HOUSEWIFE'S MANUAL by Mistress Margaret Dods (hardback £14.95)

With an introduction by Glynn Christian

Discover the world of Mistress Margaret Dods and the Cleikum Club. Mistress Dods was the founder of one of the first cookery clubs in the country and her manual, first published in 1829, includes the story of how the club was set up, over 1,000 recipes as well as hints on wine making, curing meats and making cheese. Glynn Christian says 'It is a real cookery book, a book for people who really like to eat. Comic and revelatory'. Recommended by Chat and the Glasgow Herald.

NEW FEMALE INSTRUCTOR (hardback £12.50)

First published in the 1830's the book was designed to be a practical manual aimed at turning every one of its fair readers into an intelligent and pleasing companion. It includes: dress, fashion, morals, love, courtship, duties of the married state, conduct to servants plus more than 100 pages of recipes. Lively, entertaining — the perfect gift.

THE SHARE BOOK (3rd ed) by Rosemary Burr (£5.99)

With an introduction by the Rt. Hon. Mrs. Margaret Thatcher

An up-to-date, completely revised edition of this bestselling guide to the stockmarket which has been bought by more than 50,000 people. Includes advice on every aspect of buying, selling and choosing shares. A full glossary, details of members of the Stock Exchange, Unit Trust Association and Association of Investment Trust Companies. Plus new rules on investor protection and unit trust pricing. The classic companion for anyone interested in stocks and shares.

YOUR BUSINESS IN 1992 by James Dewhurst (£6.95)

Chartered accountant, author and authority on business management, James Dewhurst has distilled his experience into this valuable addition to any businessman's library. What will the much heralded internal market in Europe mean in pratice to you and your business? The answers are inside. Includes: setting common standards, enforcing technical requirements, competing for orders from public bodies, distribution services, prospects for take-overs and mergers, new tax environment and much more.

HOMEOWNERS SURVIVAL GUIDE ed. Rosemary Burr (£3.95)

Recommended by the Financial Times, the Sun and the Times. Everything the homeowner needs to make the most of his or her investment and run their home cost effectively. Includes: choosing your home, arranging the finance, countdown to purchase, insurance, decoration, home improvement moving on and cost cutting ideas.